How To Buy And Sell

ANTIQUES

At A Profit

by
DAN SHIARAS

**in collaboration with
Fran Swarbrick**

The current values in this book should be used only as a guide. They are not intended to set prices, which vary from one section of the country to another. Auction prices as well as dealer prices vary greatly and are affected by condition as well as demand. Neither the Author nor the Publisher assumes responsibility for any losses that might be incurred as a result of consulting this guide.

ABOUT THE AUTHOR

Dan Shiaras, Grand Detour, Illinois, has been an antique dealer for 57 years and a major advertiser in "The Antique Trader" and other publications on antiques for 32 years. He is the author of two other books, "John Deere and the Billion Dollar Plow Gamble" and "How to Make Easy Money in Antiques without Even Half-way Trying."

Cover: The author with 24-inch diameter Black-eyed Susan Handel lamp, $4,500; 28-inch Steiner doll, $6,000; blue historical Staffordshire tureen, $2,500; and blue historical Staffordshire teapot, $1,500.

Additional copies of this book may be ordered from:

The author: Dan Shiaras
Box 66
Grand Detour, IL 61021

@$10.00 Add $1.00 for postage and handling.

Copyright: Dan Shiaras, 1991
ISBN: 0-9629977-0-6

To: Janet Files —
I hope you enjoy reading
my new book.
Dan Shios̄
9/17/91

**Although the incidents related in
this book are true, some names
have been changed.**

TABLE
OF
CONTENTS

Tiffany 33" "Spiderweb" lamp. Last reported sale was $375,000 in 1985 at Christie's. (The rarest lamp known.)

I dedicate this book to my wheelman

FRAN SHIARAS

Without her I could not have written it

Thank you for sharing the inscribed copy of your book with us. We look forward to enjoying it now and shall retain it for inclusion in our future Presidential collection. We sincerely appreciate your thoughtfulness and we send our best wishes to you.

Nancy and Ronald Reagan

Ronald Reagan

"Dutch" is what we call ex-President Ronald Reagan around Dixon. I mailed him a copy of "My Easy Money In Antiques" book and Nancy and he responded with this autographed photo and a thank you card.

INTRODUCTION

When I think back to the beginnings of my business years ago, it seems that it has been a long, hard road to walk. In the beginning, most people didn't care for antiques and wouldn't spend a dime for a truckload, while today antiques are cherished. It was heavy national advertising in trade papers that made me a well-known antique dealer.

During the past 30 years my customers have ranged from presidents of large city banks to captains of steamships calling me as their ships pulled out to sea. I have had the thrill of having Illinois Governor Jim Thompson write me and say how much he enjoyed my "Easy Money" book, one of five I have written.

In this book I have done my very best to share everything that has happened in passing along my 57 years' antique experience and know-how. I have not left out even a sigh or a groan at what I did right or what I did wrong.

If you are not pleased, write me and tell me why. If you are pleased, write me this, too. I'd appreciate hearing from you.

Dan Shiaras
Grand Detour, Illinois 61021

1

TO BE OR
NOT TO BE A
MAIL ORDER DEALER

Dealers are made and not born. The first step for most dealers is collecting just one type of antique. New collectors scour the house sales in the area looking over every hay rack and in every box for the one thing they collect. A few years go by, and they grow tired of buying just one collectible and begin to expand their horizon. It isn't long before the house starts looking more like an antique shop than a home, and this is when most collectors become dealers.

They have had experience and they know how to price their things, so the next thing you know, they sign a contract for a booth at a flea market. Most of the dealers I know started in business this way. When business gets good after some seasoning at local flea markets, the next decision is to shoot for the big bucks. This means signing a contract to show at the three-day Indianapolis show held twice a year or another big show. Here only the cream of antiques is allowed in the door. It is a show where each booth is inspected. No repros or repaints get by the eyes of those who look over every booth. This is what is called a quality-controlled show.

About 200 dealers from every state in the union show at the Indianapolis show. Most do not need quality control inspection because they are advanced dealers and wouldn't be caught dead showing anything but the best. But the quality control is necessary, because the show management cannot afford to have the word get out that a good customer from far away was sold a repaired piece of art glass or a doctored-up piece of period furniture.

To many of the people who attend this and other such shows, price is no object if an antique has quality. It would not be unknown for a dealer to sell out at high prices at such a show.

However, it is a long trip to the show, and the packing and unpacking of valuable glass, pottery, and china is very wearing. Wouldn't it be better for these young dealers to sell their antiques by placing ads in a trade journal, answering the phone, taking an order, receiving the money, and doing a good job of packing, then shipping by United Parcel? This is the consideration that has influenced most dealers in switching from show dealing to mail order dealing.

They didn't want any more long trips to strange

towns where you could get your throat cut for a dime, let alone a load of antiques.

Not long ago Fred Knight was doing the New York Armory show. After his $5,000 booth rent was paid for the three days and he had packed up his things, he still had $100,000 worth of antiques in his van and the trailer behind it. He made the mistake of stopping to eat a hamburger just 15 minutes outside New York City. When he looked out of the restaurant at his parking place, everything was gone. The trailer and van were found empty the next day by the New York cops. To this day not one stick of the furniture or piece of pottery has been recovered.

This is just one reason why many dealers have decided to sell out of their homes.

You also have to keep a close watch of your booth at shows. Fran and I went over to a Kane County show last winter, and as we were leaving we heard over the loudspeaker, ''Dealers, keep an eye on your booths, someone just walked away with a lamp.'' Before we could make our exit, we heard again, ''Watch out for your things, dealers, another lamp has just been stolen.''

You can try out the mail order business to see if it suits you with just one ad. If you can make up an ad about something that you know everything about A tc Z, it will be in your favor, because you will get callers who will question you on every detail of your antiques. If you feel comfortable while talking with them, then that is a go sign to continue selling by mail and over the phone. But if you consistently choke up when talking over the phone and conversing about what you have for sale, then you might be better off staying with flea markets and the big shows.

There is a lot more money in the shows than in the antique mail order business because you can put high prices on your antiques and people can walk by and pick up and handle them and fall in love with them. Then they are as good as sold.

In the mail order business you must keep your prices as low as possible to attract the reader-collector. There is no feeling or hugging with an ad. All there is is black and white description, and your words many times calls up a different image from what the buyer envisions. The next thing you see is a package at your door, and it's the one you sent out just a few days before. This rattles my nerves so much that I'm usually not well for a day afterward.

Go either way, it's up to you, young people who want to make antiques your business. You can go the flea market route, but I predict it is on its way down. I chose the mail order business, which I have regretted at times, but overall it has made good money. During the past 50 years my customers have ranged from presidents of large city banks to captains of steamships calling me as their ships pulled out to sea.

In this book I have done my best to share everything that has happened in passing along my know-how. I have not left out even a sigh or a groan at what I did right or what I did wrong. I have to tell it like it is.

2

WHAT'S NEW
IN THE
ANTIQUE BUSINESS

Repros

In order to collect something, the American public has made a complete about-face. In many instances people today are not spending money on real antiques but instead on the Depression Glass of the 30's and 40's. This is a dangerous investment.

Every six months or so I receive in the mail from a large repro company a catalogue showing all the Depression Glass patterns of past years in different colors including red. What would cost you several hundred dollars at an antique show is here in this catalogue for a few dollars.

After all, what sort of problem is there in reproducing all the scores of Depression Glass patterns? All that has to be done is make a mold of the patterns.

The reproduction of Depression Glass came to my attention about 1970 when a now huge St. Louis repro company sent me a flyer. Besides Depression Glass, they listed in their catalogue a hundred other glass collectibles that they had copied and at that time would sell to dealers only. If you went to their showroom you had to show them identification that you were a dealer. Now by ads in all the large trade papers the public is welcomed as a customer.

Reproductions have become a very lucrative business, with the unscrupulous dealer putting them on the shelves of his shop or at a flea market and not saying a word about their age. He pretends he does not know. He nabs young people much of the time. To a young couple new at collecting, all the glass in the shop or show booth looks beautiful, and they pay him good money for something he has purchased for only a few dollars. There are several books out on Depression Glass picturing and pricing the different patterns, but how is one going to tell the old from the thousands of new pieces made over the past 20 years? Even the rare cherry pattern is pictured in the repro catalogue at ridiculously low prices.

To avoid being stuck with repros in art glass, take time off to go to prestigious antique shows and memorize the way Tiffany, Steuben, Aurene, Crown Milano, and Durand signed their art glass. There are many other signatures you must learn to know if you are to start an art glass collection.

I want all the readers of this book who are prospective dealers to buy one piece of art glass that has an acid-etched signature in the pontil. When you look at this type of signature you can see there is no denying its authenticity.

It took me three years to learn if a piece of mother-of-pearl art glass was real or a repro. I forced myself to go out and buy an expensive piece and hold it and look at it almost every day in order to understand the difference.

Repros can be "signed" with counterfeit paper labels. About ten years ago a firm in Iowa started selling phony R. S. Prussia decals that you could paste on the bottom of a piece of china that looked like the original, high-priced red marked china. The decal was then smoothed over, probably with a coat of lacquer. Very few dealers and collectors caught on for several years that they were being misled. The phony R. S. Prussia was not found at major shows because there the wares were inspected by an expert before showtime.

The ruse was pulled at smaller shows and flea markets. The crooked dealers dealt in cash, so when you found out too late that you had been stuck, there was no recourse.

When the word spread around that this type of dealing was going on, everyone who had notions of bidding on R. S. Prussia would rub the red mark back and forth until nearly wearing it off to be certain that it was genuine underglaze and not a decal. If you have a delicate fingertip it is not hard to tell the real mark from the crooked mark. Rub your finger ever so softly across the red mark, and if you feel even the slightest tingle indicating roughness, forget the piece.

I know dealers who forge signatures on repros of Lalique, Verlys, etc., art glass with a jeweler's pencil. It can work if they are handy with script. You'd be surprised how many jewelers will forge a signature on a piece of art glass for you for a nominal fee.

Not long ago a law was introduced in Congress making it mandatory for glass manufacturers to sign and date all their art glass. The passage of this law would have made many dealers and collectors happy, but unfortunately it was never passed.

Where Have the Antiques Gone?

Twenty years ago you could go to an estate sale and load up a pick-up truck with fine furniture in cherry and walnut, plus fine china and glass. Today if you go to a sale you're lucky to see two or three good pieces. It seems that every other person at a sale is either a flea market dealer or a dealer of sorts. The chances of buying something right are almost nil. What has happened to the antiques that used to be easy to find?

One of the things is that there are so many flea markets and shows where people can go to check on the value of the antiques in Grandma's house, that when Grandma passes away, the self-educated relatives divide up the goodies.

If the relatives bid at sales, you might as well go to the next sale. I watched an oak hat rack sell one day for $1,450, just because heirs are a very jealous bunch and each does not want the other to get what he figures should have been willed to him in the first place.

Another reason for the few antiques at estate sales these days is that it is people who married in the 1930's whose goods are being sold, and at the time they set up housekeeping they did not buy furniture that would become antique by the 1980's.

Today if you want to buy lots of antiques you must take in nationally advertised estate collections. Here if you can stand prices from $500 to $2,000 and up per piece of glass and more for furniture, then go. Fran and I tried these sales a couple of times. I couldn't even get in a bid because the auctioneer would start out a piece of art glass at more than I could sell it for. These sales are strictly collectors' sales. Nationally advertised sales sometimes bring in bidders from 15 or 20 states, with nothing more to do than spend their money.

Dealers cannot compete with collectors, because dealers must buy at wholesale prices to make a profit. Today I stay within 50 to 75 miles of home base. There may not be many fancy antiques at these sales, but we will often come home with a wagon full of saleable items.

Sometimes Fran and I will get up early and go to two or three different sales in different parts of the county. We will look them all over and decide which one will be our best bet and then drive back to it, sometimes 50 miles.

If there is a depressed area in your region where factories have shut down, sometimes you can do well there at estate sales. Recently in Moline,

Illinois, where a factory closing and strikes have affected the economy, it was no problem to me to buy every good thing at a sale.

Going to sales today is not what it was ten years ago, as now everyone has a price guide in the car. They are ready to bid sometimes higher than the book price to get an item, and then they smirk that they have got it away from Shiaras!

The first price guide came out in 1952 and it was Warman's. I saw it by accident in an antique booth, and ordered one, and it did more for my knowledge of antiques than any other book. I memorized that book and its prices, and I became quite hard to outbid. I was cursed many times for bidding so high, but I would advertise my purchases in trade magazines for just a little under Warman's prices. I had near sell-outs on all my ads. Soon I was driving new cars every year. I kept up with Mettlach stein prices through Bob Mohr's price guide on Mettlach, which very few stein owners knew existed.

I inserted ads in all five major national antique publications asking to buy Mettlach steins. They came in by the hundreds from as far away as Germany, where G. I.'s would read the ANTIQUE TRADER in P X's. I traded my Pontiac in on a new Cadillac and began to travel in style, all because I had two great price guides.

It was no trouble selling Mettlach steins through my ads. There was a lot of big money out there waiting for me to write or call that I had some for sale.

If I tried to advertise for steins or Royal Doulton today I would get so few it would hardly pay for the ad. If you are accidentally offered one, the seller will usually have a price guide and you won't be able to make a dime. Often the seller will ask the retail price and you will not be able to make anything.

The only thing I can tell you to help out in this situation is to tell the seller that the price in the book is the RETAIL price. The real price to a dealer on the stein or Royal Doulton is 60% of the book price, and if the seller doesn't believe it, he can read it in the preface of the price guide.

With the advent of all these price guides, I quit advertising to buy antiques. All I did was sell what I bought at auctions or from individuals, and did I sell! I was able to travel from Disneyworld to the Grand Ol' Opry several times and take in the best eating places on the way. Advertising paid my way from poverty to a pleasant life. It was all done in the last 15 years.

A word of advice to all who want to succeed in the antique business and not just struggle along. Advertise. It is fun, it is profitable, and through the calls that come in you get to know how the weather is in all 50 states, even in England, Germany and India. I have received calls to buy antiques from shipboard, from the 75th floor of a New York skyscraper, and from oil rigs in the Gulf. Making good money and having fun doing it is a hard combination in life to beat.

3

THE
FOLK ART
QUILT

After supper I usually sit down at our old round oak table in the kitchen and read the classified section of the local paper to see if any antique sales are listed. One night a couple of years ago I opened the paper as usual and saw a strange caption over an antique auction announcement.

"No sale held here since 1893," the caption read. I told Fran that the place must be loaded with some great antiques. The sale was to begin at 9 a.m. on Saturday, and it was Wednesday when I read the ad, which meant that I had two days of tortured waiting ahead.

Saturday morning was bright and clear, which meant there would be a big attendance. When we got to the farm where the auction was being held, about five miles outside a nearby town, it was 8:30, and for a mile or so up and down the gravel road all available parking was taken. A neighbor waved us into a pasture parking area, which also was nearly full.

Good-bye bargains for today, I said to myself. As we walked up a slope toward the weatherbeaten house, we passed row after row of rusted-out, century-old farm machines, and old tractors with steel lugs that somehow had escaped during several wars being melted into ammunition. I heard a farmer say, "This one will bring good money today." Another guessed the tractor would bring about $10,000. I told Fran that it looked like what didn't glisten was gold. We counted five or six of those old steel-wheeled tractors made between 1910 and 1930 when the switch to rubber tires began.

We walked past antiquated machinery ranging from a one-row picker to high-wheeled wagons, and piles of old harnesses. We were heading for the house to see if any glassware or china had been put out that would appeal to us more than the old machinery that we would not even stick around to see sell.

At the house we saw an area in the yard of tables covered with pots and pans. On the center table where the good stuff was usually displayed we were surprised to see only Depression glass and a cracked art glass vase. The reason there was so little good stuff was apparent. The deceased owners had been so frugal with their money that they had used corn cobs and kindling wood in old cast-iron stoves to warm themselves with, as we could see from the number of stoves standing around.

We were just about to leave when I noticed a stylish lady standing nearby and out of curiosity struck up a conversation. I learned she was the executrix of her uncle's estate and had flown in with her husband to settle it. I asked her if she liked antiques, and she told me she hated antiques and would be glad when all the stuff was sold so she could fly back to New York.

Fran and I did a quick check of the premises to see if we had overlooked anything. On the other side of the machinery we came to piles of feed sacks. I told Fran I had learned in reading the ''Trader'' that feed sacks with advertising on them were in demand. Here were 200 stacked in piles of 50!

Then off across the pasture I noticed a pile of bright-looking quilts.

''What a hell of a place to stick quilts, where no one can see them,'' I told Fran.

When we got over to the pile and started going through them, I saw that they were either ripped or machine-made, which makes them unsaleable to a quilt collector. I could still sell them for $50 each to our lady friend in Iowa who makes little dolls and animals out of the good parts, but there was no real money in them. We call holey or machine-made quilts fit only for this purpose ''cutters.''

I dug down through the cutters and the comforters, which I would not touch with a ten-foot pole because they are just tied together and tufted with no hand work on them. I said to myself that as long as I'd sorted through that much worthless junk, I might as well go all the way to the bottom.

There at the bottom of the pile was a dated 1870 five-foot by five-foot child's hand-sewn applique quilt that wasn't supposed to be there, I assumed. It was so beautiful as well as being mint, that I nearly had one of Redd Fox's Big Ones. It was a folk art quilt with a large ferris wheel in the middle and children in different-colored cone-shaped hats all riding on different colored carousel horses. All were eating ice cream cones, and over their heads, balloons floated in the air.

The quilt was appliqued in bright-colored calico in blues and shades of red on a creamy-white background. In one corner there was an organ grinder and his monkey, in another a lady selling balloons, all done by the needle of a lady with a great imagination and without doubt the best quilter in a large area.

I quickly piled all the sad-looking comforters and quilts over the quilt that I estimated I could sell for $1,000 without a bit of trouble. Now the sweat began. When would the quilt be sold? I was hoping, as fast as possible, because old "Flintface," my Stillman Valley nemesis, had arrived on the scene, as well as Mrs. Woods, a quilt fancier from nearby. They could sniff out a rare quilt like a mouse comes to cheese. Although I had immediately walked away from the quilt pile as soon as I had discovered the rare quilt, I could see from afar that they had discovered it. I told myself that there was warfare ahead. Flintface had caused me to lose a lot of money in the previous 30 years, and she looked like she was in fine fettle to rip me off once more.

Woods, who had been in the game for only five years, could be scared out with some high bids, but not Flintface. She lived and breathed early American folk art in her shop and at all the antique shows where she had shown over the last decade. She was a hardened veteran just as I was and when we hit head-on in a battle to the death it was usually this old "biddy" who would walk away with the prize, overbidding its true value by $300 or $400. I knew she would bid $1,000 just to keep the rare folk art quilt out of my hands. I knew I was close to losing the most folksy quilt ever made.

"What can I do?" I asked Fran. "They have torn the pile apart and they have seen the quilt."

Presently I walked back to the pile of quilts to be certain the folk art quilt was still there. I couldn't find it anywhere! I tore everything apart, quilts, comforters, and all, strewing them all over the ground. No quilt. It was gone. One of those two _ has stuck it under her coat and walked off with it, I said to myself. I KNEW they were sticky-fingered. It couldn't have gotten away any other way.

Then I said to myself, I'm going up by the house and see if the executrix is still there, and ask her if by any chance she took the quilt. When I heard what she said, I nearly collapsed. She told me she had taken it because it was the only thing out of her uncle's house that she liked.

I told her a touching story about how much I would have liked it for my grandson (not yet born or even expected).

"I will pay you $75 for it," I said.

When the executrix heard $75 for just a small quilt, she told me she would go inside the house and ask her husband about selling it. In the meantime I had folded $75 in cash inside my fist just in case she did come back with the quilt.

I couldn't believe my eyes when out of the house she came with the quilt in her hands. Her husband, she said, had no use for the quilt and would rather sell it than keep it.

The deal was made, and no sooner made than I stepped over to Fran and told her to go quickly to our wagon and bury the priceless quilt so deep somewhere than none would spot it. I told her, "Hide it like only you know how so that even if someone breaks a window, it is safe."

After the quilt was safely hidden, Fran and I heaved a sigh of relief. Over across the pasture where the quilts were, both Flintface and old lady Woods were throwing quilts all over the ground, in the air, and back in the brush, looking for the great quilt that they had anticipated taking home with them. I could see the tearing and clawing as the already holey, ripped quilts kept rolling. First they'd scatter them all over the ground, and then they would throw the comforters in the bushes. Then one by one they would place each quilt on top of another, hoping that magically the rare quilt would pop out of the deck. Finally after half an hour they gave up, leaving the quilt area looking like a battlefield.

The time had come to sell the quilts. I bought all 11 of the holey, shredded, torn quilts for under $15 apiece. I had my ready market for them. These quilts cleared about $300 after being U.P.'d to my Iowa customer.

I then set myself to buy the piles of feed sacks, which were clean and had bright-colored advertising on about half of them. Not knowing the feed sack business, I made a mistake and bought all the piles at the same price. I long ago sold the advertising sacks at a good profit, but the 100 or so plain ones are still piled up in my basement. If anyone reading this needs some feed sacks, they can have all or part at 50 cents each.

When I got home and looked over the child's bedroom quilt again, I loved it so much that I hung it up on the wall in the hallway. That way I could admire this great work of the quilter's art every day.

One day I needed some money, and to get it I ran a photo of the quilt in my ad along with other photos of fine antiques. A keen-eyed obstetrician from Arizona spotted it and called me and ordered it. I had put a stiff price of $750 on it, never thinking anyone could hack that price for a small child's quilt. I could see by the doctor's letterhead that he had a clinic, and I can only assume that the folk art quilt with its carousel-riders became a wall-hanging in his waiting room.

After the sale that turned up the folk art quilt was over, I learned that the average price paid for the five old rusted-out tractors was $5,000. I nearly decided to retire from the mail order antique business and go into the junk farm machinery business. The older and junkier farm implements looked, the higher the price was that day. Of course the collectors who bought them put in weeks and months rejuvenating them to add them to their collections. I say, everyone to his own poison. My poison is fine oil paintings, Oriental rugs, period American furniture, beautiful dolls, and hand-made quilts. art pottery + art glass.

Circa 1870 5'6" x 4'6" hand-made applique crib quilt, current value $1,250 to $1,500.

4

THE ELUSIVE
MECHANICAL
BANK

Some years ago I read in the Dixon paper about a sale to be held just south of town. There was nothing in the antique line advertised, but I thought since it was only a few minutes from my house and since I needed something to do while Fran got her hair coiffed, that I would look it over.

I dropped Fran off at the beauty parlor and then headed south for Ben Miles' place. He had dropped over dead a few weeks before while mowing his lawn. He didn't believe in anything but muscle power, and at his age it dropped him.

Ben never in all the years the neighbors knew him threw anything away. He remained single with only a couple of relatives scattered around the state. Going to a tavern for a beer was his only relaxation and enjoyment, and after a couple, he'd spit out his hatred of women. He was an old miser, and figured women were out to steal his money.

With thoughts like these, I can see why he stayed single, unbathed, unshaven, and wore overalls that needed washing the year before.

These recollections were what made me hurry down to the Miles farm. You never know what a man of 80 might have stashed away. Since the auctioneers had advertised only machinery and a short sale, other antique hunters were not apt to be out and it could be my lucky day.

When I arrived at the sale there weren't over 30 cars parked there, although I was late. This meant there wasn't a good line of machinery for sale. Ben was only farming 40 acres, and ten of that was in garden. The auctioneer had already sold everything on the hay rack, which was dishes and pots and pans, and had gone over to the machinery. When he sold that he would finish up the sale in the house.

There were some pieces of oak furniture that might sell well, I thought, as I snooped around the old house. I kept poking around, and as I pulled up one of the shades in the living room, I damn near collapsed, because standing on the window ledge was the rarest mechanical bank known. The last known sale of it had been made a few years before for $50,000.

I picked up what we call the Old Woman in the Shoe mechanical bank. I placed a coin in the slot and pulled the lever. The old lady sitting up high on the cast iron shoe with stick in hand punished her children moving toward her. Her bright yellow bonnet was in good paint, and all the way down to the top of the shoe she sat in, she was also mint paint. The whole thing looked so mint that if you didn't know your banks like I do after 30 years of buying and selling, you would pass up the bank as a new repro and let it sit on the window sill. This is what the auctioneer no doubt did in hauling Ben's few pots and pans to the hay rack, leaving the bank with the furniture and thinking it would be sold to some kid for $15 or $20.

This is the average price that repro mechanical banks bring at auctions today. They fool a lot of buyers and sometimes skyrocket in price as high as $50.

I prayed that the crowd there that day would be average and not contain some experts. Could it be possible, I asked God, that at long last I could buy a $50,000 bank for $20?

My watch read 3 p.m., and I knew by now my Fran would be standing outside her beauty shop looking up and down the street for me, and I anticipated I would really catch hell.

The last piece of Ben's machinery was finally sold and the small crowd of local buyers followed the auctioneer into the house. My heart was pounding fast. I didn't see one person in the crowd that had the potential of interest in antiques. There was a mild interest in the worn-out furniture but that was all. Half of the crowd had not even come in the house, only about 15.

The auctioneer had sold several pieces of the furniture and was getting closer to the pulled-down shade that hid a fortune, when in came a lady in high heels and a mink coat that was a stranger to the area.

Here comes trouble, I said to myself.

The lady whispered something to the auctioneer, and he pointed to the pulled-down shade. She walked quickly to the window and pulled out the $50,000 bank right in front of my nose and put it in a tote bag. She walked snappily out the door with her heels clacking.

I waited a few minutes, recovering from the shock, and then said to the auctioneer, "What happened to the bank I was waiting to bid on?"

"Do you know who that lady was?" the auctioneer replied. She's Ben's niece from Sterling, and since I didn't advertise the sale in the Sterling paper, she only found out about it at the last minute from a friend. She said Ben had told her that if anything ever happened to him to be sure and get the bank, because it was worth at least $500."

I left the auction in a hurry, but not before I got the niece's name and address from the auctioneer. I then waited impatiently a week or so, not wanting to seem too anxious, and then contacted her, asking if she would care to sell her bank.

She had already sold it at a small sale near Tampico! She didn't get anywhere nearly what her uncle thought it was worth! It brought only $20 along with OTHER REPROS!

It has been five years since this incident happened, and I still do not know whether the bank was old or a reproduction. It looked so mint, how could it have been old?

And yet, there had been no children to play with it. And the niece had been told when she was a little girl of the worth of the bank. If it had been a repro, Ben would not have made that statement. I think it is more possible that it was old than new.

The memory of the rarest bank in the world that I never got to bid on will always haunt me.

The rarest mechanical bank known, the Old Woman in the Shoe, $250,000. When coin is placed in the slot and lever pulled, old lady punishes children.

5

I THOUGHT
CAPONE'S OLD GANG
WAS ALL DEAD

For years I had heard that a gangster lived on a farm on the outskirts of a nearby town. When my brother and I would occassionally be drinking beer in a tavern there, the farmers would turn the talk to Orlamon. They'd relate that it was rumored he was the wheelman for Capone but had fallen into disfavor with Big Al and was told to get out of Chicago. If he didn't get out fast they'd be hanging a ticket on his toe down at the Cook County morgue. Or he would be fitted with a pair of knee-high cement boots and dropped in the Chicago River.

"Just get out of town, Orlamon. You've got 24 hours."

Orlamon knew that what "Scarface" Capone said, he meant. Orlamon took his wife and car and pulled out of ritzy Oak Park, leaving all his furnishings and his home, never to go back. All he took with him were two Oriental rugs. All else was lost.

This was in the 1920's when Capone ruled both Cicero rackets, booze and prostitution. He also had spread his power into parts of Chicago. This Orlamon had accumulated a large amount of money driving Capone around on his hold-ups.

What I don't know is why he picked out a small, four-room house just a couple of miles out of a tiny town to move to, when he could have driven to Florida or California. He was not long in his small frame house before he started to spread out and bought first one big farm and then another until he owned better than 600 acres of ground close to his dwelling. This he rented out to tenants. They weren't the ones who talked about him.

When Fran and I had lunch at the Ramada Inn in Dixon we used to see this hard, high-cheek-boned, steely-eyed man with the brim of his Panama hat pulled down come in to have lunch with his diminutive wife. They would not mix with anyone and rarely did I ever see Orlamon smile.

Not knowing at that time who this was, I asked the manager about him, who told me the wheel-man report.

"Don't fool around with him. He's bad medicine," said the manager. "I don't even want to say hello to him."

One day in 1980 when Nate and I were partners, I was sitting in my house when I heard a knock on the breezeway door. It was the beginning of the most fantastic adventure of my life.

An old man whom I had never seen before said, "I read in the Dixon paper where you buy Oriental rugs and pay a 10% finder's fee. Is this still in effect? Do you still pay 10% if I tell you where there are two old Oriental rugs? I crated them up over 40 years ago."

I told him I'd have a look and got his address. It was one mile out of the tiny hamlet of Pine Point on the south side of the slab, he told me.

"It is the only big white frame house out there, so you can't miss it. The name is Al Lieber, in case you get lost."

I got in touch with Nate and he got excited that two Oriental rugs were for sale so close to Dixon.

"Let's go down tomorrow," Nate said. "I'll bring the van. They may have a lot more to sell."

I met Nate the next day and we drove down to my tipster's house. When I went into the house I saw he and his brother were living just like they had lived back in the 30's. An old cast iron cooking stove with wood piled beside it furnished the heating. It was a dirty house and I wanted out fast. Bachelors leave their houses go, I know, but these brothers overdid it. Al led the way to the rugs, which I thought had to be junk by his way of living. But it turned out we were going to another farm as we followed Al in his pick-up through several turns and finally up a long, limestone driveway to a small, one-car garage that lay west of a little frame house about 100 feet.

We then waited until Al got the owner of the rugs to back his car out. When the owner came into view I almost got a heart attack. I whispered to Nate,

"Do you know who that man is? That is Gangster Orlamon that used to belong to the Capone mob in Cicero. He was the wheelman in getaways until Capone told him to get out of town!"

This did not bother Nate a bit. He's a nervy little guy, and I think if Orlamon had come out of his house with a machine gun it wouldn't have phased gutsy Nate. Orlamon as he approached us showed his age but he was still hard-looking like Humphrey Bogart in his gangster movies. He got into his new Cadillac in the one-car garage. I could tell he was failing because it took him three tries to back out. First he'd hit one side of the garage and then the other.

I said to Al, "Where in hell are the rugs you told me about?" as we looked into an empty garage. Al pointed up toward the ceiling and asked if we saw the two long boxes above.

"That's where the rugs I crated 40 years ago are. They're heavy, so let's all three of us take them down off their hooks."

We all tugged and lifted up and then down on both crates. One of them weighed at least 100 pounds more than the other.

"Let's uncrate the heavy one first," said Nate. I was beginning to think that if there were any good rugs around, the rats would have gotten them or dry rot taken its toll.

When Al took a long pry wrench to the box, I could see something red and flowered inside, with a sheen like a cat's back. This is when I really got excited.

When the whole crate was laid open, there rolled up was a mint-looking, finely-woven rug. Nate started to unroll it, and it was so long that it stretched out into the muddy corn field next to the garage. We rerolled it and stretched it out on the driveway. It was 24 feet long and a prime circa 1910 Sarouk worth easily $5,000 at that time.

Then we got going on the other crate with Nate helping rip the boards off in his anxiety to see what kind of luck we'd have in this crate. When it lay open, before us was a beautiful Aubusson-type gold with much floral design Chinese 9 x 12 rug with its original Marshall Field tag on it. It was truly beautiful with all its wide floral border and large medallion of flowers in the center. Easily a $750 to $1,000 rug, I told Nate. Chinese rugs were not hot on the market then as they still aren't. But still, I told Nate, we did have one hell of a great rug.

We had Al go up and bring Orlamon back down to look at the rolled-up rugs and ask him what he wanted for them. He said from the door that if we did not know what they were worth to us, not to bother him while he was eating breakfast.

I said, "Oh, oh, Nate, we're in good shape here. He doesn't give a damn what they are worth. He is more interested in eating his breakfast. I guess we might just as well go to the door again and see what we can buy them for. Let's get it over and get out of here."

I remembered all the gangster stories I'd heard about this man and I figured if we didn't pay him a good price he might shoot us. When I knocked on the door, Mrs. Orlamon started to talk to me through the screen door. She never once asked her husband one thing about the rugs. It was just me and Mrs. Orlamon.

Just as I was going to offer a big price for them and had my mouth half open, Nate ducked in front of me and said we'd pay $600 for them. I damn near fell over at his nerve. He sure had guts to offer $600 for $6,000 worth of rugs when I was going to offer $2,500.

Mrs. Orlamon said, "I certainly will not sell those rugs for $600. I paid more than that at Marshall Field's for the gold one."

Then came the most astonishing conclusion to a deal I ever heard of or ever will again. She said, "Make it $650 and you can have them."

I passed her the money through a crack in the screen door and thanked her. Nate ran like a madman down to the rugs and paid the old bachelor $65 for locating the rugs. With his help Nate lifted the biggest rug into his van. It was a good thing he decided to drive it, because the palace-sized antique Sarouk took up a good part of the van's floor. And then quickly the thick, heavy Chinese rug was loaded and we sped out of there in high gear before we would get a machine gun bullet through our back window as Orlamon finished his breakfast and found out he had only received $650 for his Oak Park home's rugs.

Nate took both rugs to his house. He was then the same way as he had been with the baseball cards. He wanted to hold everything, and all I held was the bag. He got in touch with an Oriental rug dealer he'd met at one of the large rug auctions

in New York and told him what he had. The eager
Persian was at Nate's door the next day. A Persian
can smell out an Oriental rug just like a rat can
smell cheese. A deal was made to sell the Sarouk
without even consulting me. The Persian had con-
vinced Nate that the Sarouk was not a Sarouk but
a painted rug, which means the red color that made
the sheen so beautiful was just red paint put on
by artists in Persia and now by imported girl
painters and repair girls brought over from Persia.
Some place in New York had as many as a dozen
girls repairing rugs by reweaving them and repaint-
ing them, he told Nate. Nate bought the thief's story
and sold a rug for $3,000 that I could easily have
sold to my Chicago and New York buyers for $5,500.

When Nate sprung the news on me, I wilted.

"Why, Nate, did you sell my rug that I had
advertised for without talking it over?"

"I thought it was a good price, and besides
it was taking up both rooms in the house. Glori
ordered me to sell it."

"Now what are we going to do about the Chinese rug before you decide to give IT away, too?"

"You said it was worth $750, and since Glori
and I like it, we'll just pay you your price for the
rug and keep it."

Nate kept the rug just long enough to get tired
of it. When he tried to sell it to the New York Persian who bought the other rug, he got a negative
response.

"No buy Chinese rugs. Must be old 1880 Chinese Canton if I buy."

I reminded Nate there was going to be a big

Oriental rug sale at Chicago the next Sunday, and suggested he could sell it privately in the parking lot.

That day we saw a young Persian from New York buy all the 80 or 90 rugs that were sold. Even the ruler of Chicago's rug empire just shook his head at what was being paid. After the sale was over and Simon, the New Yorker, had paid off a half dozen Persians for not bidding against him, Nate told him about our 9 x 12 Chinese rug outside. We all went out and under the parking lot lights Simon went over every inch of it. He looked for holes and repairs, and finally deciding we were selling him a good Chinese rug, the haggling began. Nate wanted $1,000 and Simon told him $650. Finally the price of $750 was agreed upon.

Simon told us both that he needed lots of rugs, good ones, and that started a new chapter in my life in the exciting Oriental rug business.

6

FROM
PICKER
TO DEALER

When I got my discharge from the army I had to find something to do. I couldn't find a job that suited me and must have gone through a dozen or more until one day a friend asked me to drive along to a weekly livestock sale at the small town of Chana, Illinois. When we got there I noticed two or three hayracks standing outside the sale barn piled high with both junk and antiques. The farmers would bring in anything they didn't need anymore. Among the items I saw some valuable old brass car horns and copper tea kettles with dovetailing down their sides and big copper apple butter kettle made in the same way indicating they were joined by a blacksmith and not by a machine.

For five cents and ten cents I bought a lot of antiques, and it was then that it dawned on me what

I was going to do for the next 30 years of my life. I would give up to a degree my stamp and coin dealing that I had begun at ten or 11 years of age and concentrate on becoming a livestock dealer where there were not one but two ways to make "Easy Money." I would buy antiques outside and then go into the auction barn and buy anything that walked and looked like it could make a buck, utilizing the building that Dad had given me for use as a livestock holding building and advertising for livestock in the area papers.

I never missed selling what I advertised but once. One of my customers said he felt he had to buy the pigs I had to sell because of the long face I put on when he said he'd think it over.

Farmers used to like hearing that the three or four loads of 500 to 600-pound whiteface or angus steers or heifers had come out of the Kansas or Nebraska sandhills because those were always good-doing cattle once they were put on full feed. Farmers are some of the fairest and squarest group of people on God's green earth. They were so isolated from each other that they went to sales or came to me to just jaw awhile. It never failed that once they'd step onto my stockyards they'd buy 100 head of feeder pigs, a dozen piggy sows, 30 or more close-up ewes, or a load of cattle. I even had close-up dairy cows and heifers for sale that bumped up close to calving time. (With one punch of your clenched fist you could bump the cow's calf inside.)

After that fateful day in Chana in the late summer of 1945 I went out and bought an old Dodge two-ton truck with an 18-foot stock rack and I was

off and running to six livestock auction sales each
week in different small towns in the northern part
of the state. I chose the ones that had the most junk
piled up to sell, because it was there I made lick
after lick from discarded antiques. There were sometimes beautiful Kentucky rifles on the rack with
their maker's names and beautiful engraved patch-
boxes that I'd buy for $50 or $60, now worth $1,000
or more.

Also, Fran and I would go to juicy-sounding
antique sales on Sundays, and that rounded out my
week of seven sales each week for over 20 years.

Viola, Illinois, 125 miles from home, had the
biggest sale barn in the state, and I never failed to
be there on Wednesdays. Farmers would not only
bring in thrifty feeder pigs and all else, but the
whole front of this monster barn was loaded down
with junk. It was great fun digging into all that stuff
hoping to get lucky and spot a choice antique to
buy for 25 cents or less. My big truck cab was my
travelling antique salesroom full of items that I'd
sell to dealers. They got to know me as a ''picker''
and trusted me that I wouldn't stick them with a
repro. I had several shops in every direction that I'd
stop and sell my wares to, taking only the kind they
liked and specialized in.

At the Kewanee, Illinois sale, 2,000 feeder pigs
would be sold each Friday, and outside a separate
auctioneer would sell long rows of junk, crates of
chickens and ducks, ponies, big motor boats, sad-
dles, and you name it for over an hour. Kewanee
is in the heart of Henry County, called the hog capital of the world because more pigs are raised there

than any other place. I'd never fail to sell one of three dealers that had shops in Kewanee my entire load of antiques that I'd stacked up in my cab clear to the roof.

It was there in Kewanee in May of 1957 that I saw a sign go up over the windows of a corner store building that said "Antique Trader," heralding the start of a new four-page monthly antique paper. I bought the first issue and kept it a year or two. Now the "Trader," moved to Dubuque, Iowa, is the most widely read antique publication.

I began running ads in the "Trader" beginning with issue #2 until 1970. With 7,000 auctions under my belt I began to concentrate on specialty antiques that I'd advertise for in several national publications. I got my share of everything I advertised for and became what I believe was the leading Mettlach stein dealer, Royal Doulton dealer, and Indian rug buyer in the U.S. Fran and I would attend roughly 200 auction sales a year, bringing my tally of attended auctions to about 9,000.

7

THE UNADVERTISED
THEODORE ROOSEVELT
LETTERS

In July of 1986 I went to a warehouse sale in Freeport, Illinois. It had been advertised that a lot of books would be sold at this sale from an old-money estate, that of the former owners of a Freeport newspaper. The men who do the loading for the auctioneers told me that a big van-load of the finest antiques from this estate had already been loaded and were on their way to a relative in the East. There had been two Tiffany lamps in the 20-room mansion of the newspaper publisher, and lots of fine glassware, sterling flatware, and tea services. All that was left in the warehouse was buzzard bait, as far as I could see.

It was not until the auction was half over that it was announced that some Theodore Roosevelt letters were to be sold. The wife of the clerk had found

them two or three days before the sale while leaf-
ing through a book. The relatives had missed something after all! The clerk's wife had found a Coolidge
letter as well. But neither the auctioneer nor anyone on the auction staff had considered the letters
valuable enough to advertise.

When the first letter was held up, I thought I
was going to have to fight for it, since a Rockford
book dealer was at the auction. However, he dropped
out at $155, and so it went with all five Roosevelt
letters. All were sold to me in the $150 range. I
bought the Coolidge letter for $110.

Shortly after I had bought the letters, the auctioneer got down off his stand, and passing by me,
whispered, ''Were they really worth that much,
Dan?''

I knew by then that my day was made and my
trip to Freeport not so unproductive as it had looked.

The sale had progressed about half way through
the rot gut stuff that remained when the auctioneer
suddenly announced that it would be continued the
following Saturday, since the crowd had thinned out
and he was not getting the prices he wanted. It was
the first time I had ever seen an auctioneer stop an
estate sale. The sale had been stopped just as the
auctioneer was coming close to four bound volumes
of Harper's Weekly covering the Civil War years. As
disgusted as I was at this postponement, it gave me
a chance to call a dealer in the East whom I believed
would be interested in the volumes. My buyer told
me he would pay $300 per bound volume. I told
him that the bindings were shot.

''That makes no difference,'' he said. ''We tear

them all apart anyway and sell them page by page for the steel-engraved battle scenes.''

I went back to the second part of the sale loaded with advice on the thousand-page volumes. Once more the book dealer, who had returned for the same items, and I went at it tooth and nail. The first volume sold to me for $165. That meant $135 profit. The next two, which had torn bindings, sold to me for $125, $135, and $85. I took off with my books and called my man the minute I got home. He promptly sent me $1200 for my find.

As soon as I had time, I read the Roosevelt letters, and found that although Roosevelt may have been a president who carried a big stick, he was a soft-hearted man who loved little homeless waifs and most of all, his own children.

The Roosevelt letters were written from 1910 to 1912 on the stationary of the ''Outlook'' magazine, to which Roosevelt was a contributing editor. Roosevelt had left the presidency in 1909 after serving nearly two terms.

The letters looked like they were typed by Roosevelt himself and had many corrections in pen. All were written to a lady in the newspaper publisher's family who had apparently been active in the cause of social welfare legislation and had also sent Roosevelt a short story.

In the longest letter Roosevelt wrote:

''I loved the short story of married life, and shall show it to Mrs. Roosevelt. Oh! How well I remember small figures in the little bed next to us looking steadily over the railing, and if they detected the slightest movement on my part instantly swarming over with, 'Now Father, we would like a story!'

". . . I still remember vividly one morning when the whole family seemed to be in various stages of the measles and I lay down on the sofa beside Ted's bed in what was the improvised nursery for the two children who were getting better.

"Having, as I felt, won the right to repose by a story, I said, 'Now Ted, Father has told you a story and he thinks he would like to get to sleep for awhile,' to which Ted cordially responded, 'Alright, and Ted will play the organ!'—which he proceeded to do at a distance of two feet from my head."

In another letter Roosevelt wrote, "In every kind of life the greatest happiness only comes where there's a chance for great unhappiness. But how sincerely I despise the cold or timid or selfish souls who dare not try 'the great adventure' because it is given to no human being to be certain of joy and not of sorrow."

In still another letter Roosevelt anticipated social welfare legislation, writing, "Of course I most emphatically and cordially approve of pensioning mothers under the circumstances you name. A pension given to such a mother, the mother of a large family, who had to be both father and mother. . . is as much a matter of right as any pension given to the most deserving soldier. It was a pure oversight that the Progressive platform did not specialize in the social insurance clause."

I contacted two autograph buyers in the East by sending them Xeroxes of the Roosevelt and Coolidge letters. The first buyer I contacted bid a wonderful price for the five Roosevelt letters. I mailed them to his offices in Boston and soon the agreed-upon check arrived. It made me smile as I recalled the auctioneer's question to me as to whether the letters were ''really worth that much.'' The auctioneer will never know how much the letters were sold for nor will anyone else. It was part of my agreement with the buyer to keep the sale price confidential.

The Coolidge letter was also sold in the East, but to another buyer. The Coolidge letter was written three months after Coolidge entered the White House. In it he tells his correspondent that he supports her efforts to bring relief to the starving children of Germany. I received $275 for the Coolidge letter.

I will never forget the small sale that turned out to be more exciting than a hurricane. You never know in this business where lightning will strike. That is what causes me to go to three and four sales a week. Something super can turn up that no one else knows the value of.

8

LICK-LIPPER'S
TWO-DAY
ESTATE SALE

For many years I used to park my cattle truck at least once a week on a side street in Sterling beside the home of an elderly lady named Miss Sarah. She had inherited the most beautiful circa 1890 house in the area, and it was loaded down with fine antiques and paintings, plus a 144-piece setting for 12 of Haviland Schleiger #19 or Silver Anniversary,

Every time I'd stop at Miss Sarah's house to see what I could buy, I'd also walk across the street to talk to a lady I nicknamed Lick-lipper, because she was always licking her lips due to diabetes, I later found out. Her house was even more beautiful inside than Sarah's, but hadn't been painted for so long that it had become dingy-looking. It even had a covered carriage drive near the front door where in

the old days guests could be let out and keep dry
in case of rain. I always thought that when I built
my mansion, I'd build such an entry-way.

Sarah would always sell me something, but all
Lick-lipper wanted to do was talk. Whenever I'd
mention buying the Oriental rugs on her floors,
she'd say, "Maybe sometime, but not now."

It was the same way with the Victorian marble-
topped bedroom sets in all five bedrooms. I would
say, "Since you're not using them, why not take the
money and take a trip or buy some designer clothing with the money?"

The answer I would get was, "Oh, Dan, they've
been in the family so long that I think I'd better keep
them." Then she would add that all the really old
things were out in the carriage house in back. Could
I see them? No, it was locked up and everything was
too dirty. Perhaps later.

Since there were no children, I didn't know
who was going to luck in on this marvelous collection. One day Lick-lipper relented and sold me a
decorated Mt. Washington vase for $150, but she
never got over crabbing about selling it.

"I miss it," she'd say. "Will you bring it back?—
I'll give you your money back."

I couldn't bring it back, as I had already sold
it. I didn't keep antiques long in the 1960's, with
four hungry mouths at the table not counting Fran's
and mine.

Years went by, and Miss Sarah died after I had
bought many of the antiques in her house. Then Fran
read in the obituaries that Lick-lipper had died, too.

She was no sooner cold in her grave than a

niece came in from Chicago and took over. She had Auctioneer Osgood from Lanark come in and inventory what was to be sold. Osgood listed all the offerings of the two-day auction in the newspaper, and it sounded fabulous.

On the day of the sale when I arrived, the Persians from Chicago had already pulled up and parked in front of the house. They took a lot of big rugs out of their cars and soon the street was full of Oriental carpets. The Persian sellers tried to outshout each other about what each rug was worth. The other half which was doing the buying also bartered at the tops of their voices that "Your price too high, I give you so much."

I, too, was one of the sellers once I got there. I had got stuck with $1,600-worth of Hamadan and Lilihan carpets at Janesville, Wisconsin, the month before, and I wanted in the worst way to unload them to someone. But the wary Persians did not even consider buying them. They knew they were hard to sell.

All this noise carried to the east side of Licklipper's house, where Osgood had his van parked. It wasn't long before someone told Osgood about the street being blocked by some people selling each other Oriental rugs. Osgood rushed out to the side of the yard that overlooked the street and told everyone to get the rugs loaded and out of the way. I loaded up my rugs in a hurry, because I knew Osgood didn't warn anyone twice before taking action.

It was then that all five Persian rug buyers huddled together with me and Nate, who had also come to the sale, and picked Nate to bid on the rugs for everyone. This was to make the rugs look like they were worthless to professional rug buyers.

As the sale began, we were all in for a let-down. I asked Osgood, "Where in the hell did all the marble-topped furniture go?"

He said the niece had a last-minute change of mind and had decided to sell only the junk, and keep all the good stuff. The good stuff had been loaded into a van during five hours of the night before.

The 15 quilts in mint condition that I had wanted to bid on and were advertised to be sold the first day never did come out of the house. Osgood said he couldn't do anything about it.

"If the heir wants to load them up after I've advertised them, then I can't stop her."

The five rug dealers plus Nate and myself waited to see the Oriental collection that had been nationally advertised, sell. The rugs were antique and worn, but still valuable.

Nate bought all the rugs as they were handed out of the house. He did a good job of faking it, as he just loved to bid and show off his knowledge. To make it convincing that he had bought all the rugs himself, he hauled them all out in back to the street alone. The crowd would never guess that he was just a front for the Persians.

When a dirty white one with a blue border and a blue medallion came out looking like it wasn't worth a dime, Sol Mokali from Chicago and New York City stepped up behind Nate and said "Buy this one. She's a good one."

After all the rugs had been sold, Nate took the Persians out to the back street, and there began the second auction for the rugs, with a considerable number of room-size and throw rugs lying in the middle of the cement street. The hollering and arguing disturbed some of the neighbors, one of whom was ill and complained. All of a sudden Osgood came out madder than hell and told the gang to move away from the street or he'd call the police.

Nate told the group he knew a man who lived nearby who would let his yard be used, so the auxiliary auction moved over there and went on for over an hour. Finally Sol bid $8,000 on all the rugs, and since they had cost only $2,000, he had to pay off all his partners in crime the difference, which was $6,000 or $1,500 apiece.

Nate came back after the bidding was over and handed me a $100 bill for my share for not bidding initially.

"What did you get?" I asked Nate.

"I only got $100, too, and it sure wasn't worth it. I'll never get involved with a bunch of Persian rug buyers again."

Sol, on the other hand, was very happy that he had bought all the rugs for $8,000.

"What was so good about that white one you wanted?" I asked. "It looked like junk."

"That, Dan, is an 1880 rare white Canton rug, hand-made in China. Most Canton rugs are blue, but this was a rare rug and I'll sell it for good money in New York after I have it washed and hung up in my Fifth Avenue shop.''

All the hard-core dealers and collectors had hung around until the sale ended, hoping something would fall out of heaven to pay for their day. The house was empty and all the wicker that had been in the big, two-door carriage-house-garage was sold. Osgood had no doubt said to himself that he was getting the sale over in good time. Another half hour, and it would have been pitch dark.

I can still remember the look on Osgood's face when someone hollered out, ''When are you going to sell the things up over the garage? I was up there today, and it is full of old trunks and a bobsled.''

All the dealers and collectors pricked up their ears. Osgood got a neighbor to bring a ladder, and with a flashlight he slowly climbed up into the garage attic.

''Whoa, there! Wait a MINUTE!'' he yelled. ''This sale isn't over yet! I need a few drop cords and some lights!''

The show got on the road as soon as neighbors had brought lights. The first thing I remember being let down was an eight-foot bob sled with bright red paint and gold stencilling. Fritzie, one of my Dixon rivals, bought it for $375 and immediately climbed on it and squealed with delight, trying to make other bidders envious.

More and more good things came out of the attic. I remembered, then, what Lick-lipper had said about all the good old stuff being in the carriage house.

The hump-backed trunks were unloaded of dolls and old-fashioned clothing. A collision took place between Fritzie and myself and two other dealers over the dolls. I can still see Fritzie with six dolls tucked under each arm as she topped all bids.

Other trunks were emptied of lace-loaded ladies' undergarments, and ball gowns with bustles.

If Lip-licker had only sold at auction just what was in the carriage-house before she died, she could have lived in comfort.

If "Lick-lipper" had only sold just her beautiful dolls while she was living, her life would have been much happier. The Bru and Jumeau French dolls in the photo sell from $15,000 to $25,000 each. Photo Courtesy of Coleman's Encyclopedia of Dolls.

9

THE
UNOPENED
BOX

It has been about five years ago that I read in one of my newspapers of what sounded like a juicy farm sale just north of Sterling. It was a long sale bill, but it did not even mention what was going to be one of the most unbelievably profitable items I had ever bought.

Since there wasn't another interesting sale advertised in the half-dozen papers we subscribe to, I told my wheel-man that we would go to Sterling. You never know what these sales may kick out.

When we arrived it looked like a country fair was in progress to see cars already parked a mile down the gravel road and out in a cow pasture, where men with canes were directing traffic. We parked and then dodged cow pies in summer heat that neared 90 degrees before 10 a.m., and finally reached the sale grounds. I could see at a glance what had brought out so many. There was another smaller pasture on the other side of the sale grounds which was full of people looking at row after row of old farm machinery, surreys, and half a dozen wagons. Three old tractors were equipped with steel lug wheels. There were a 1911 Waterloo Boy and two makes I'd never heard of before. All the attention was being given to the Waterloo Boy which had been made in Waterloo, Iowa, and its company bought out in 1913 by the giant John Deere Company which at that time needed a tractor to add to their diversified machinery line. There were only a few made and they were the forerunners of the John Deere tractor.

How this farm family could have kept all this equipment for so long without sending it to the junk yard was hard to understand. Fran and I walked to the yard to look at what we thought might be antique dishes on six hay racks, but there was little else but old cooking utensils and junk. One rack had stacks of old farming magazines such as FARMER'S WIFE and SUCCESSFUL FARMING, but these have never sold in my ads even though from the 1910 to 1930 era. I asked around who the people were that owned all the old farm stuff and was told that Mennonites had lived there for generations and had passed away, causing the sale of everything including baled hay and even a flock of laying hens.

The sale of the steel-lugged Waterloo was the No. 1 attraction, yet until I got there I had never even seen or heard too much about that model. By the looks of the differently dressed men showing interest in it, it would be a toss-up whether it would go to Moline to the John Deere Museum or to a rich tractor collector. The sale was not nationally advertised by Emil Shade, the auctioneer. He didn't know how much bigger a crowd he would have gotten had he let it out that a Waterloo Boy plus the two other tractors were to be sold on that muggy day.

After looking over the entire sale, I couldn't see more than one or two things that interested me. There was a row of brass gas lighting fixtures propped up against the fence, and an old steel De Laval advertising sign showing a pretty milkmaid with arms around a cow's neck that was a high priced sign. It would sell sharply higher than the $400 sign I had sold to the Ranch house restaurant in Bureau, Illinois, ten years before and which still hangs there. This one would probably bring me $1,200. I asked Fran if she wanted to go home or wait till Shade went through six hayracks and got to the sign. Fran wanted to do her usual thing and go through each room of the imposing old home, which had not known paint since its first coat when it was built. I passed on looking at the house and walked back down along the hay racks and scrutinized each carefully for a sleeper, but found none. I gave one of my first loves and best money makers, the old magazines, another look, but there wasn't one bundle stacked up that gave any indication that it would sell to collectors. So I went over to a big shade tree by the house and planted myself under it. The hot sun did not bother the farmers, who had all come in straw hats and were gathered around the farm machinery. The city people couldn't take the sun any more than I and had all ducked for the shade.

Fran finally came back from her tour of the house and the hay racks and asked me to come down and look at what she had found.

"There is a tall box tied up with binder twine and it says 'tractors' on it," Fran said. My heart jumped about six beats because I knew how valuable old tractor brochures could be. I'd sold a few, and sometimes I got as much as $30 each for them even if they were no earlier than 1920's and up to 1935 John Deere and McCormick Deering brochures.

Back at the hay rack, I moved the bailing string over far enough so that I could see that six or seven kinds of tractor brochures were in the cardboard box that had been selected long before to neatly fit the brochures. When I pulled the box open a bit and got a better look, my heart nearly stopped. The tall carton was full of steel-lugged tractor brochures, and on the very top was a 1911 Case steam engine catalogue easily worth $100 to $150 to a collector. I quickly closed up the carton.

The carton was sitting on what I figured was the No. 2 rack in selling order. Shade started the sale promptly at 10 a.m., but instead of getting over to me, he started at the other end of the racks, and I kept my fingers crossed that some farmer wouldn't untie the box. When Shade finally got to the rack where the magazines were, he had his help scatter out the bundles of farm magazines with 50 to a bundle and said the top bidder could have the choice of any package. I didn't want to run the bidding up too high and tip my hand that something good was on the rack, so I hardly bid against a lady dealer, figuring she would not be interested in tractor brochures, and sure enough, she picked a bunch of early sewing magazines with a black man Cream of Wheat ad on the back of one. This kind of bidding nearly cleaned the rack, while for some unknown reason the tractor box was still not untied. There were collectors of old farm magazines there, but not once did they ask Shade to open the 2-1/2 foot-tall box.

I then asked Emil, "How about $50 for choice of anything left on the rack?" Emil and I were not what you'd call buddies after all the sales of his I'd gone to and his jealousy that I made money at all of them by knowing what to bid on and how high to go. He ignored me at first, but since he was not getting much for the remaining bundles, he said he would go along with my suggestion for one time. Then I'll be damned if he didn't take other bids, when usually my bid would have been accepted as top. With just a few stacks of magazines left, a man to the side of me raised my bid and soon we were up past $100. I said to myself, there is someone else who knows about the tractor brochures. But my neighbor dropped out at $100 and I had the choice of the rack at $110. Shade had a shocked look when I picked the only unopened box that was left.

I told Fran to pick up the box and haul it across the road to our car and lock it in, then cover the box. I told her there was a lot of money in what she had found and in what I and everyone else had missed. I would go pay up and not buy anything else, as I saw one of my most hated rivals hanging around the DeLaval sign, and lampman Tom Whitehall had just arrived, so that took care of the lamp parts. I never bid against him because he had bought thousands of dollars worth of lamps from me and I didn't want to spoil our good relationship. He had even bought the scenic gone with the wind lamp for $600 in 1968 that had originally come from the General Grant home in Galena, and he still had it. It showed a shepherd tending his flock top and bottom.

I stayed just long enough to see the Waterloo Boy sell. It was all rusted and strange-looking, but this did not stop furious bidding that raised by thousands at a time until the price got to $30,000. The dumbfounded Shade sold it to a tractor collector from not over ten miles from my house who had 100 or more steel-lugged tractors housed in his new steel building.

I told myself, here is the man who will buy my tractor brochures.

My wheelman and I headed back to Grand Detour. When I opened the box I counted 130 tractor brochures plus six large Case and Rumbley steam tractor catalogues dating to 1900. All were in mint condition. As I went slowly through the brochures, every company name known to man showed in this rare collection. A lot of the brochures were in color and not faded after 60 years.

After I had looked them over I did not know what price to put on them. I called my nearby tractor collector anyway and asked if he would like to buy some of them. He said he knew he would, since there were two Waterloo Boy brochures in the lot. He also collected old steam tractors and had three or four, so he would like to look at my catalogues of Case and Rumbley, which were the thickest in the lot.

The collector picked out 17 brochures and catalogues and handed me $1,500. I nearly fell over at this high offer. Everyone has his own collecting fever.

It wasn't long before I met someone who did the steam power shows, and he paid me what I asked for the remaining 100-plus tractor, steel-lugged tractor, and machinery catalogues and fold-out color brochures on tractors. When it was all over I had sold the box of brochures and catalogues for over $3,000. If Emil Shade knew this he would have a stroke. It has been over five years since he made a big mistake by not opening the only tied-up box on that rack.

Fran had finally unearthed something to make some serious money instead of just pointing out to me things I'd already seen.

10

THE
OLD CROW
DECOYS

Born on a farm in Putnam County, Illinois, Charlie Perdew carved his first decoys when he was fourteen. These first blue bills, made from charred pieces of an old bed, were used on nearby sawmill lakes. It was also here that he shot birds for the Chicago market.

A year later Perdew went to Chicago to work in a meat packing plant, and soon after, as a carpenter in the building of the Columbian Exposition of 1893. At this time he attended classes in painting at the Art Institute.

Returning permanently to Henry in 1898, he began a gunsmithy and bicycle livery and repair shop, in addition to carving duck and crow decoys. In 1909 he patented his crow call, which is considered to be an heirloom by those fortunate enough to possess one.

A decoy much admired and sought after today is the Perdew crow, especially the early ones. Later he tended to carve them slimmer, but the demand is still there with an average Perdew crow decoy changing hands at $600 to $800. This genius at crow and game bird decoys died in 1963 at 89 years of age. It was estimated he carved over 25,000 decoys, and is considered to be the finest decoy maker of all time if not the most prolific.

I had no idea that the sale Clip Ferguson had advertised for a July day a few years ago would have anything to do with Charlie Perdew. But the sale sounded promising. It was at a house that had been deserted and boarded up for years. This is the type of sale I like to go to, because what was inside 40 years before when the house was boarded up was probably not known as antique. There might be art glass pieces signed Tiffany or Quezal, or even a rare, signed Tiffany table lamp.

What the auctioneer had dragged out of that house was indeed a sight to see. All was rotted due to a leaking roof. No wonder the heirs from Ohio had not even bothered to come. All I heard was 25 cent and 50 cent bids. People were hauling furniture to their cars that was falling to pieces behind them.

I then noticed a small peeked barn in the back that needed looking into. Some of these barns, once used for horses and wagons, still remained next to older Dixon houses.

When I walked into the barn, I saw Nick Simon,

our local scavenger, had been hired to clean out the barn. When I saw what he was doing I wished for a stiff drink of whiskey. This man who had tinkered around with antiques for side-line money was up in the loft and was throwing down crow decoys from a distance of 15 feet onto the cement floor. What I saw on the floor would make an insane person sane, or vice versa. This antique-dealer-on-the-side had ruined a pile of $600 to $800 Perdew duck decoys. All had their base spikes intact for sticking into tree branches to attract crows so local sportsmen could shoot them.

By a quick count I came up with 15 broken-billed, tails-gone decoys worth at least $5,000 to $6,000, and he was still dropping them down.

I called up, "You Nut, don't you know those crow decoys are valuable? You have ruined a small fortune!"

There were only two or three left when I told him this, and these he brought down himself. He did not believe me, however, that such a decoy, all black, could be worth good money. I told Nick to go put the decoys on a table in the yard so I could bid on them.

We waited for an hour for Clip to start to sell the decoys. I didn't see one person in the crowd that would even remotely think of bidding on them, so I figured a $1 bid would take all four of the best ones. I had no sooner thought this wonderful thought when up walked Mel Spender, who was a local store manager.

What is this young rascal doing here, I thought to myself, when he is supposed to be minding the store? Mel had been outbidding me for years on Oriental rugs, quilts, and furniture, but surely, I told myself, he didn't know anything about decoys.

That is where I figured wrong, because from all the antique shows he attended, Mel did know a lot about them. He bid me up to $85 on first choice and $65 each for all the rest. He caused me to bid almost $300 more for the decoys than I would have had to pay if Clip had moved to the decoy table before the canning jar table. I saw Mel smirk as he visited with a friend. He had done it to me again.

Nick nearly passed out at these prices. The decoys had been left by the heirs to be hauled away to the junk pile.

Well, I had four Charlie Perdew decoys, I said to myself. They would make some money even if they were bruised a bit.

When I got home I called the Minnesota Lodge of a big decoy dealer and collector whose father used to carve ducks at the same time Charlie did at Spring Valley along the Illinois Flyway. I explained that I had just missed buying 15 or more Perdew crow decoys, and when I told him what had happened, I think I heard him cry. He loved Perdew's beautiful hand-carved and hand-painted decoys, and I do believe if he could have been at the sale he might have pulverized Nick for what a nutty thing he had done.

The collector told me, ''Don't bother to repair them. Any dealer or collector that hands out $600 to $800 for one of Charlie's decoys is not so dumb that he won't spot your repairs. Send them up to me on consignment and I'll try my best to sell them at a profit. All I want is 20% commission for my work.

I packed the crow decoys up, and in no time at all the U.P.S. brought them back. A note inside said they were not Perdew decoys at all, but just average decoys carved by an average carver.

Here I had cursed out Nick for damaging, and cursed Mel for putting the screws to me on, what turned out to be just common decoys.

Now I didn't know what to do with them. Who would I sell them to?

I took them to Fred Knight. Fred would buy about anything, especially if it was shown to him shortly before one of his Sunday auctions.

Fred assumed the decoys were rare, like Mel and I had. He paid me $40 apiece. When Sunday came I went to the sale, because I wanted to see what happened to my crows.

When it came time to sell them, there was silence. Many or most all of this gallery had never seen a crow decoy. All they had even seen were beautifully carved duck decoys with beautiful feather painting. For those four junk decoys Fred could not get a bid, no matter if he reached for the microphone and cried 50 times. I hated to see Fred lose $160 right after I had lost $190. Both of us thought at one time or another that they were Perdew decoys, as Mel Spender had thought.

Fred never did tell me what happened to my crows. I know one thing for certain, if they didn't sell at the Sunday sale, he would take them along on his show circuit. If he talked to little old ladies long enough, they would end up buying not only the crows but part of his booth.

11

ON YOUR MARK,
GET SET, GO
FOR THE SALE BATTLE

Before I go to an auction, I study the sale bill item by item. Anything that interests me I circle, and then I go back and study it as to current prices, and even call people in the business to ask if something I am doubtful about bidding on is still saleable, or is dead.

It takes me two days or longer to decide which antiques I want to bid on and how much to bid. This is just an educated guess in most instances.

I say an educated guess, because many times the man who makes out the sale bill neglects to mention the chips, the gouges, and missing parts of the juicier items. He also fails to tell the sale bill reader that at the last moment a niece pulled into town and claimed the better pieces, which she maintained Auntie had promised her, and made such a damn fuss that the auctioneer let her take what she wanted.

The people driving 100 or more miles for those ''juicies'' look astounded when they are told they won't be in the sale. Most ring men and auctioneers keep quiet about this last-minute robbery of the sale. I, personally, get so mad that I cannot speak for some time. I choke up and turn red as a beet, my Fran tells me, and if I have a tie on, my neck swells out over my collar an inch.

In my car I carry at least 20 price guides on everything from dolls through toys to beer cans. You don't know what you may run into that wasn't listed at a sale. But if you have your travelling library of antique information with you, all you have to do is run to your car before the sale starts and look up the current price of what you have seen.

Just recently I saw a 12-inch Crown Milano vase at a Dixon sale, and hurried to my car to see what it was pegged at. I nearly fell over when I saw it described to a T and listed at $2,750.

I waited all day for the sale to get started. When the ring man finally picked up the gorgeous vase with three angels on it, he looked at it stupidly and then handed it up to Wilson, the clerk, and pointed out to him the Crown Milano mark on the base. Wilson was a dealer and a clerk, both, but he still did not know what was staring him in the face. Wilson then passed the vase over to Chet Hathaway, the auctioneer, to see if he could identify the museum-quality art glass vase. Chet shook his head, and said, ''Let's sell it.''

Chet got a bid of $10 from me. He then bid $20 himself. When I bid $30, to my amazement he said

"Sold!" I kept a straight face in front of the gallery of Chet, Wilson, and the ring man, but I could have screamed with glee. I had just put in my hip pocket $3,000 for $30, simply because I knew my glass and all of its marks.

This does not come easily. You must study a subject for years before you are proficient enough to walk around without an identification book in your pocket, and you will never be able to do without your travelling library.

In my case this includes the Official Price Guide on Royal Doulton Figurines and Tobies, listing every one made and their prices, which can range up to $10,000 for a White Churchill and $7,500 for a Hatless Drake toby jug. It's the same way with Royal Doulton figurines, of which there are 2,900. An early-number figurine can put thousands in your pocket if you spot one and have checked it out in your car library.

I want to stress again studying your sale bill ahead of time to be ready for what it offers. You may then be prepared to hit a $10,000 jackpot.

New dealers are not in a position to outbid an experienced mail order dealer at an auction. This is because, if the mail order dealer is like me, he has a large group of potential buyers to sell to through ads. The best thing for old and new dealers to do when they meet me at a sale is to not stick around and waste their time.

I hate being the guy at sales who is accused of being hoggish and not allowing anyone else to buy anything worthwhile. Many times I know I am $200 or $300 over on something juicy, but I will not give up to the opposition. I do this to teach them a lesson that after this they should not stick around when they see me. I get them to thinking I'm just plain nutty and throwing my money away like a drunken sailor.

There is method to my madness, and it is beginning to work. It took me 20 years to scare the other bidders out, and now I am beginning to reap the harvest. Without these bothersome people bidding on all that is good, the good things are beginning to come my way at reasonable prices. I hate to do this but I must, because it is the only way I can make up for all the poundings I have taken along the way.

Young dealers might just as well fold up their tents and go home from most auctions, as there are people in the gallery or house sale crowd that have more money to spend on antiques than Carter has pills. Or dealers like me will ruin it for them.

There is one dealer in Rockford who is my nemesis and my only opposition in that city of 200,000. He is at every sale where there is something good. He never gets anything bought at a reasonable price, but then, neither do I, the reason being that he bids $100, $200, or $300 over what a rare piece of glass or some other antique is worth.

12

THE
ROYAL FLEMISH
VASE

At a local weekly auction sale which I attend regularly, I noticed not too long ago a decorated, 12-inch-tall vase stacked among a table full of nondescript glassware and silver plate. The vase was decorated with small berries and vines. I asked myself what such a vase was doing in amongst all the milk bottles and pop bottles. I pulled it up gently, turning my back as I did so on the strong-arm lady among local antique dealers who was in the audience. I did not want Bubbles, as her husband called her, to see me look for a signature in the pontil.

Sure enough, the vase was signed with a small red reversed R and an F interlocking. I recognized the signature immediately as being Royal Flemish, one of the four or five big names in art glass made in the 1880's. It was patented by the Mt. Washington Glass Co.

All of Country Cal's Thursday sales are night sales, so you can prepare yourself to be up until midnight to get something you want. While we waited I said aside to Fran that it was strange that Bubbles, who knows all art glass marks and current prices, had not looked at the very valuable Royal Flemish vase. Since it was diminutive, perhaps it had escaped her ever-roving eyes.

At that time Bubbles and her husband did all the big-city shows, and in doing all the big shows you become superior in your knowledge. In all honesty, I was jealous of Bubbles and her expertise.

When the time came to sell the vase—late in the evening as it was bound to be—Cal got down from his stand and walked over to the collection of milk and pop bottles where the Royal Flemish worth $1,500 stood. He gave this one of the five or six most valuable pieces of art glass in the U.S. a loud clank by pulling a $2 pop bottle from behind it. I did not dare ask to look at the vase to see if it was damaged with Bubbles sitting close by.

Cal then picked up the Royal Flemish vase, and spotting the reversed RF signature, passed the vase to the clerk to see what he thought. It was obvious that it meant nothing to the clerk. He shook his head and threw out his arms, meaning to sell it. Bidding on one of the most valuable pieces of glass ever made in this country 100 years ago was about to begin, as my heart pounded so hard I thought it would come right out of my chest.

The auctioneer held up the vase, worth $1,500,

and asked the crowd, "What am I bid for this 'bottle?'" It is hard to believe that the crowd, including strong-arm Bubbles, would not start the bidding over the price of an antique milk bottle. Finally I looked at Cal, whom I have done a lot of favors for, and spread all my fingers (held at waist level where they could not be seen by others) two times, signifying $20. He understood the bid and started the vase at $20. For awhile it looked like he might have to sweeten the pot with more bottles to get any further bids. Then, since it was getting late and he was probably anxious to get home, he knocked the vase down to me for my one bid.

This vase is now in my wife's show case of art glass. I could sell it in a minute for $1,750, decorated as it is with little bunches of berries and vines. Had it been decorated with geese in flight in relief or with gold and silver coins the size of half dollars, then it would bring $3,000.

The Mt. Washington Glass Co. in the 1880's made four of the highest-priced and rarest art glass vases ever made, one of which was Royal Flemish. Others are Crown Milano, decorated Burmese, acid cut-back in both pink and blue, and the king of art glass, Plated Amberina. A water pitcher in Plated Amberina will sell quickly at $4,000 and $5,000. Plated Amberina comes in many shapes, such as vases, tumblers, etc. The reason it is so high-priced is because it had a tendency to pop and break while being fired at the factory. It would also break with a change in temperature while in your cupboard. Very little of it is left.

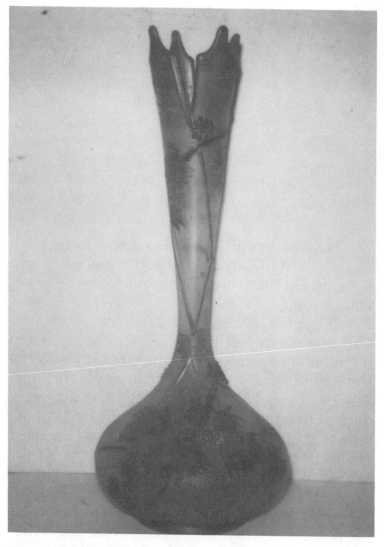

My rare signed 10-inch Royal Flemish vase, $1,750.00 — $2,000.

13

TAG
SALES

Tag sales are called estate sales in many areas. So they are, but they differ greatly from estate auctions. In tag sales, every item in a house is tagged with a price.

To get the best buys you must get in line first. This may require getting up at 2 a.m. to get in line. If it is bitter winter weather, you'd better wear some battery-heated underwear and carry a pint of hooch in your hip pocket, or risk freezing to death before the first ticket is handed out at 7 a.m. Some antique buyers go up the night before, park, and exchange places in the line all night long.

Then you have about an hour and a half to get yourself full of ham and eggs and a gallon of coffee. You must be back in your #1 position by 9 a.m. because that's when your ticket is checked. When it is accepted you run into the house at high speed followed by probably nine others who scatter about grabbing hold of everything that looks good. It is almost like a football game the way everyone stamps each other and charges at tables full of fine dishes trying to holler "I want this" to partly deaf sales helpers.

When the dishes you want have been marked with your number you gallop up or down flights of steps to grab crocks or quilts.

After fifteen minutes, the next group is let in. This is the way it goes all day until 2 p.m., when everything is marked down and the same thing is gone through the next day. The tag sale crew goes on selling at a slower pace the second day. The goodies have all been snatched. By the third day you can almost name your price for anything left. After the third day, all that remains is sold to some auction house for a bid so low that the lady in charge of the tag sale pretends to faint.

At the tag sale it took three days of hard work on the part of five or six women working at minimum wage to sell what an auctioneer who knows his business could have sold for higher prices in 4-1/2 hours.

I firmly believe in the auction way to sell your estate or collection. Most tag sale managers don't know their antique prices, so they either put too high a price on an object, preventing its sale, or give something really valuable away. You can't be pricing rare antiques or even the mediocre kinds with only three or four years' experience. You have to have a lifetime at this business to know what is rare, semi-rare, or pure junk that looks rare.

14

THE
JACKSON
PORTRAITS

The year was 1960 when I decided to show Fran my old home town of Galena that I had left in a hurry with Dad and Mom in the dead of night 34 years before. Mom did not see opportunity for her two sons in the sleepy old town that had nothing going for it but an old, beat-up main street and nearly-starving merchants. The town had nearly died long before when the lead mines shut down. The Galena River, once crowded with steamboats, could not even float a good-sized fishing boat.

I was coming back as well to see if I could find Vern Vincent, who had been the one bright spot in my young life. He was my tutor in buying and selling fine U.S. stamps. He owned without a doubt the finest collection I had ever seen of U.S. stamps both in sheet form, plate block form, and in mounted, rare single sets, going all the way back to 1847 when the first U.S. 5-cent and 10-cent stamps were minted. I was hungry to see Vern to find if he still had all or part of his collection. I belonged to the Dixon-Sterling Stamp Club at the time with several advanced collectors. I figured if I could buy Vern's collection I could leave all the other collectors in our club behind.

As I drove into Galena my heart jumped a bit, because there was my old school up on the hill, and there was the river where I had spent all my waking hours in the summer fishing for channel cat. The town didn't look as bad as when we'd left it in the heart of the Depression. In fact it looked busy. This was quite a switch.

I went from tavern to tavern asking for Vernon without any luck. I then tried the eating places, and finally at one end of Main Street a cafe owner told me that Vern came to eat dinner at his place every day. He told me that Vern lived up at the end of Bench Street with a Mrs. Margaret Anna.

"I don't know if they are married or if Vern just rooms there," he said.

I drove to the last house on Bench Street, which was badly in need of paint. When I knocked on the door a diminutive elderly lady answered. She said Mr. Vincent was asleep in his room but invited me in. I decided to go in and wait for him to wake up. I introduced myself as a home-town boy whose parents used to run the Cozy Cafe down on Main Street. Margaret Anna then recollected that she used to visit with my mother when she wheeled me past in my baby carriage.

"I used to look down at you, Danny, and wish you were mine," Margaret Anna said. "I loved you that much when you were a baby."

When I had walked into the house I got the shock of my life because there directly before me were a pair of the most beautiful portraits in gilt frames that I'd ever seen. Here in Galena in an old, unpainted frame house stood a pair of portraits that looked to be a match for any pictured in ANTIQUES magazine and which sold at the New York auctions for $100,000 and over.

I stepped back out the door and called for Fran to come in. Fran had the same look of amazement as she saw the portraits hanging in the living room on either side of the big cast iron parlor heating stove. One was of a man in a black suit and the other of an old lady in a bonnet.

I then began to look farther, and everywhere I saw nothing but beauty and the best of days gone by. When we started to visit and I began to pry a bit, I found out that this sweet old lady was the last of the Jackson line whose grandfather had built in 1859 the home later given to U. S. Grant. All of the paintings that hung on the walls in this unpainted house, and all of the furniture in it including that in attic and basement, had at one time adorned the mansion her grandfather had built. He had sold it to Galena citizens to give to General Grant on his triumphant return from the Civil War to his hometown of Galena. The citizens turned over the keys to the Jackson mansion to Grant on August 15, 1865, Margaret told us. Her grandfather had fallen on hard times and was forced to sell his house. He moved to a modest frame home, taking his furnishings with him.

The paintings on the wall were of his father and mother, Margaret said. The father was a surgeon in Vienna, Maryland. He and his wife passed away within months of one another and their son, Alexander (the builder of the mansion), went back to Maryland to settle the estate and bring a load of priceless jewelry, paintings on ivory of family members, and larger paintings to Illinois. The paintings on the wall were two of the paintings brought back and were painted in pastel around 1830 or 1840 by a good artist, Margaret said.

Alexander Jackson's father was a wealthy man and could afford the best artist in the East.

"All the furniture you see around the house and the marble-top tables were all in the mansion," Margaret said. "The same with the walnut beds and marble-top matching dressers and commodes, which I have stored up in the attic." "I inherited them in 1900 when my father passed away. I was only a little girl at the time, but I was named as his sole heir."

I ate all this up. About this time Vern woke up and came down to see who was talking with Margaret. When I introduced myself I could see Vern relax a bit. It didn't take me long to get the picture that Vern considered this his private domain, hoping to inherit all that was in it and pass it on to his son. With that in mind he had kept all Galenaites, I heard, out of the house, fearing that they might persuade Margaret to sell them its contents.

This buying job was left to me, and I did it

swiftly, forgetting all about the stamps. The fact
that Margaret knew me opened the door. She felt
I was in some way one of her own kin of which
there were none left. She was also anxious that
nothing of hers be sold publicly to townspeople
after her death.

I made about eight or nine trips to see Margaret. There was always a waiting period of a few
minutes before I was allowed to buy antiques or
valuables. Vern and Margaret would discuss the
sale, and in the end I would always be allowed
to buy whatever I wanted. Vern did not exactly like
this, but at the same time he liked the money I
was paying. He would put it in his pocket and Margaret would not receive one cent. I bought gold
heirloom jewelry, and the pastel paintings. Fran and
I carried them out of the house as a nosy neighbor
across the street kept tab on us from an upstairs
window. We also bought all the cut glass, R. S.
Prussia, and the bedroom sets in the attic. We
bought priceless framed "silks" containing President Andrew Jackson's printed speech dated 1838
and other speeches. Dr. Jackson, the subject of one
of the portraits, had served under Andrew Jackson
at the Battle of New Orleans and so distinguished
himself operating under fire that he was sent the
silks after Jackson became president. The President
also sent the doctor a steel engraving of himself
at the Hermitage about 3-1/2 feet tall. I bought all
of this.

Some of it is now at the Hermitage and a good
part of what I bought is now in Grant's Home as
a donation that the curator was very thankful to

receive from me. One gift was the only known picture of Alexander Jackson, who built the mansion. This was a daguerrotype in a gold locket. Margaret sold it to me in 1964 and I kept it until 1983. It now reposes in a permanent setting in the Grant Home where all 250,000 yearly visitors may see it. I also donated the only known plans of the Grant Home.

Vern died almost ten years before Margaret passed away. I then had to deal with her lady caretaker who ran a boarding house for elderly ladies. I was once more lucky. This lady loved money even more than Vern had. She, too, remembered my dad's restaurant. This was the in I needed to go through the house without any problems and divide what remained, I paying for my half and the caretaker taking half to apply on the boarding bills that Margaret had run up.

When Margaret passed away the Galena dealers and collectors could not wait for the sale of the contents of her house. They knew it was loaded from attic to basement. When the sale day arrived, they descended like locusts to clean out the antiques. I heard later from a dealer that all that was left for the Galena-ites was what Margaret told me she wanted sold locally of her heirlooms, and that was nothing. The caretaker and I had made her wish come true that nothing of value would be sold in a cheap way on the street. All that was left for the dumbfounded Galena-ites was newspapers, magazines, canned goods, and pots and pans.

My dealer friend said the word was soon whispered through the crowd that a dealer from Dixon had gyped Margaret out of every antique she owned. Pretty soon they had blown up the story so high that if I had come to the sale I think my life would have been in jeopardy. Galena-ites did not take to the idea that an out-of-towner had cleaned out Galena antiques that should have remained in Galena museums and private collections. I guarantee you I didn't go back to my old home town until a long enough time had elapsed for all the heat to have cooled down, because the red necks who didn't get in on part of the swag would have cold-cocked me with a sap.

In 1984 I was about to donate the two great pastel paintings to the state, since they had hung in the Grant home for six years, when my wife objected. Because of the affection she had developed for Margaret Anna she could not let these last mementoes of a gracious lady go. Fran's words to me were, "If the paintings go, I go.

"I don't care if you promised the curator of Grant's Home that you would have the paintings up there next month so they could go on display for the Fall Festival. You have gone too far already in giving and selling to museums the priceless things Margaret Anna sold you, and what are the thanks you get from them?"

I had had an Eastern art expert evaluate the paintings by mail in the meantime. His appraisal was $10,000. This would be deducted from my income tax. I thought this was a clever way to save money.

About this time a prominent local artist, Lois Franz, was invited to come and look at the paintings. She saw in minutes that they were the work of an accomplished artist. Lois begged me not to donate the paintings at least until she had a chance to evaluate them and try to determine whom they were the work of, as they could be worth a great deal of money if it turned out they were the work of a recognized artist. The difficulty in determining this was that the paintings were unsigned.

The second thing that Lois noticed was that the paintings bordered on the primitive. The portrait of Mrs. Jackson, in particular, had a gaunt and ghostly look with staring eyes. Louis had the feeling that the pastels reflected the artist's primitive style, and that if she saw other paintings by the same artist, she would recognize them. She said the pastels were probably done by a travelling artist, because pastels could be finished in a few hours, while oils took longer. Numerous pastels were done in the early 1800's, although they were not as popular as oils, and some pastels hang in Mt. Vernon.

For days Lois looked through books and magazines to try to find similar works of art to no avail. Among the magazines she went through were about 100 copies of ANTIQUES which I gave her. One day she called in excitement and said that in a 1975 issue she had found a 20-page spread of the paintings of Sheldon Peck, an early 19th century artist, that reminded her of my pastel paintings. We put the spread up next to my portraits and you could see at a glance that Mrs. Jackson's lace collar was identical to the collars of several of Peck's subjects. Dr. Jackson's suit collar and his suit were also nearly identical with those of some of Peck's subjects. Not only did Dr. Jackson's facial characteristics resemble a portrait in the magazine, you would swear you were looking at the same person.

Also, all of Peck's painting's original frames were similar in size to those of my paintings. We also noticed that all of Peck's subjects pictured had drooping mouths as did my portraits. They had piercing eyes, prominent brows, small, pointed noses, large eyes, and the women all had angular, haunted-looking faces similar to Mrs. Jackson's. The almost scary similarity of the William Welch portrait in ANTIQUES to Dr. Jackson was the living proof to me that Peck was the artist who painted wealthy Dr. Jackson and his wife. Mr. Peck's distinctive style was reflected to a T in the Jackson portraits. Also, Sheldon Peck never signed his works.

We then decided to take the old backing off one of the pastels, hoping to find a signature or some other information. What we found was an 1836 Baltimore newspaper.

While this did not settle the question of the artist, it did serve to date the portraits. Sheldon Peck remained a possibility as the artist, because we knew he was in the East and in New York state at that time. He could have travelled in Maryland as an itinerant artist, as he did later in Illinois.

I studied everything about the pastels as closely as I could, because it meant the difference in owning a pair of $10,000 portraits or a pair of $60,000 portraits. I shudder to think that I almost donated $60,000 to the state when all the thanks I would have received was thank-you and goodbye. The portraits might not even have been displayed. They are now in a vault, and my Fran is much more pleasant to live with than if I had given them away.

Top, Dr. William Jackson, 1838, and Anna Jackson, 1838, parents of Alexander James Jackson, attributed to great Vermont artist Sheldon Peck and appraised at $40,000—author's collection.
Bottom, only known photo of Alexander James Jackson, builder of Grant Home in Galena, IL, 1858 - priceless.

15

SELLING
HUBBY'S COLLECTIONS
WITHOUT PERMISSION

When you run an ad for specific antiques and get a letter from, say, 50 miles away, this means go and have a look. No matter how strange and unpromising the call or letter, follow up every one. Even a call about something you don't want can lead to a whole bevy of antiques.

Back in 1980 when Nate Ross and I were partners, he ran an ad in the Freeport paper asking for Oriental rugs. A new ad and a new name can bring out new sellers, and this time the net had caught what seemed to be a most unpromising prospect from the letter received. It merely said that the seller had a few old Oriental throw rugs, and to stop and see them if ever in the Forreston area, adding that the sellers were hardly ever at home.

It was a week-end, and I stopped to see Nate

to find out if anything was new. I found him watching a baseball game. He showed me the unpromising letter and said he was not going to follow up on it. I always had been a great believer in running down every response, the reason being that it furnished a chance to get into a house, and you might be able to buy other antiques, beside the ones for sale, that you might spot and ask about. So I called the number given in the letter. When a lady answered, I said I was Nate, and had received her letter and would like to drive up and see her throw rugs. She told me they didn't amount to much, and there were only seven or eight of them. I said I could not be there for an hour, as I had other rugs to look at.

This was mainly a ploy to make it appear that my ad had caused other Oriental rug owners to decide to sell.

When Fran and I pulled up at the house, we saw it was the just-right kind of house from the 1900 era. It had two storys, which meant lots of rooms to look through. I knocked at the door and asked if I could bring Fran in, too. Fran just loved looking through such an older home.

As I looked at the rugs, which were piled on a porch, I saw they were common Hamadons and Lilihans that don't sell for much over $60 to $70. But as I peeled the pile back, what stared me in the face but an antique Keshan mint six-foot-plus throw rug.

Here was a rug whose fine wool shone in the light like the fur of a well-fed kitten. It dated about 1880. It was woven from wool of the high mountain sheep of Persia. When I flipped the corner of it over casually with my foot I could see it was so thickly woven you couldn't begin to see where one knot started and the next ended.

Here, I told myself, is a $5,000.00 throw rug, as I piled all the dusty and half-worn ones on top of it. Out of sight, out of mind, was my theory. Let Mrs. Sanders look at the coarsely-woven backs of the dirty rugs that needed a good washing. I was expecting her to come back with a big price because she had told me the rugs had been in the family for a long time, she thought for at least 100 years, as she started to trace back the family's ancestry.

"I'm going to ask a good price for them, Mr. Ross, or give them to the children," my seller said. "I'd have to have at least $300 for them or I won't sell."

I nearly keeled over to hear this, because I could sell the six badly-woven rugs for $300, and then the prize Keshan would be all profit.

I kept a straight face and tried to "jew" the Forreston lady down, making it seem there wasn't any profit in the rugs at $300.

"I'll tell you what I'll do, Mrs. Sanders," I said. "I'll give you $250 cash for them and haul them out," and with this I produced five $50 bills.

Money talks. If you don't believe it, just wave this much money at a party who is selling something that he or she believes is junk, and see what happens.

Mrs. Sanders looked at the money and replied, "Let's split the difference. If you give me $275, they're yours and you can haul them out of here before my husband gets home and gives me hell for selling his relations' priceless rugs. Just dust-collectors is what they have been up in the attic all these years. I'm sure he has forgotten all about them.''

I paid the $275 in a reluctant way and told Fran to load the rugs up, as we had other places to go to look at rugs. Fran made it in two trips, and when the wagon was safely locked up, she came back in to say good-bye to Mrs. Sanders.

"Say, Mr. Ross," said Mrs. Sanders, "do you buy Haviland dishes?"

My heart jumped a beat, because Haviland was one of my specialties over the years and I had bought and sold dozens of sets of these expensive dishes. Mrs. Sanders took me to the kitchen and opened up the doors of her cupboard, and there was a partial set of Ranson #1. It is pure white and stamped on the bottom, Haviland and Co., in green. It was sent to this country by the thousands of sets in the 1900-1910 era undecorated but still quite handsome.

If a set is decorated at the factory it has a red mark on it as well that says Limoges, France.

Fran told Mrs. Sanders she'd help her take the Haviland out, and there was just six of everything plus a covered dish and a large platter, around 40 or 50 pieces in all. Mrs. Sanders told us that when her mother passed away some years back she and her sister divided the set.

"It isn't of any use to me anymore," she said. "We don't entertain much, and a six-place setting doesn't go very far around the table at Thanksgiving and Christmas. What will you give me for it, Mr. Ross?''

I looked at the set and told her that since the set was all white and not decorated it was not in demand like other sets. I told her that people who didn't have much money at the turn of the Century bought all-white Haviland because it was much cheaper since no work had to go into decorating it.

I'll give you $150 for the Haviland," I said.

"Sold," she said. "Let's get it packed before Mr. Sanders gets home."

Fran soon had it packed perfectly in the couple of boxes that we always carry in the car, plus plenty of newspapers, in case of any eventuality. Out the door she went carrying the dishes, and then back for one more box, as I paid Mrs. Sanders her $150.

What Mrs. Sanders did not know is that Ranson #1 is one of the best-selling Haviland "patterns" and that each cup and saucer was worth $30 while the dinner plates sold for $15. I totalled in my head what I could get for the partial set from a Haviland replacement center, and I came up with $300 to $350. This made a couple of hundred dollars fringe benefit for driving up to look when Nate was too lazy to come, prefering to watch the baseball game that he'd bet on.

To any who may think I was buying too low, I quote from advice to small business people carried in a 1978 newspaper: "In the retail world, a product that costs $1 to make sells for $2 wholesale and $4 retail, the price doubling at every turn." Of course, sometimes I more than double my money, but this is balanced by the times I lose money!

More goodies, including cut glass bowls, were pulled out from drawers. All were bought fairly but at a price I knew at the same time would make me good money.

"Say, Mr. Ross, do you buy old electric trains? We've got a set that my husband owned back when he was a boy in the 20's."

I said to myself, *This means it has to be a standard gauge train worth at least $400 or $500!* As Mrs. Sanders, Fran, and I went up to the attic, my heart began to pound because I could smell money being made up there. It was dusty and had cobwebs all over, a just-right setting to find something really interesting. For five minutes Mrs. Sanders could not find the train, and then finally she said, "Here it is behind this pile of suitcases." When the last suitcase had been moved out of the way, there stood a big box, and on it was written, Lionel Train. These words scrawled across the cardboard box set my heart beating even harder.

When I took the strings off the large carton, I could hardly believe my eyes. All of the 1925 train set was in its original cartons that came with the set direct from the Lionel factory. When I took out the cars, I saw they were not 10-inch or 14-inch cars in standard gauge as I was accustomed to seeing and buying. Rather, they were eight-inch cars with a smaller engine, but all mint with not a scratch on them.

"What will you give me for this train?" Mrs. Sanders asked. I stood back and pretended to figure out with a pencil and paper what I could give her. Since there were seven cars and an engine,

I told her the best I could do would be $100. I figured $10 each for each car and $30 for the engine, and then I might be able to sell it for $10 or $25 profit if I could find a buyer, I said.

"It's not the size of the big cars of the '20's," I told her. "Some of them string out to nine feet in length." Mrs. Sanders accepted every word I said, and told me to pack it up before Mr. Sanders got there and she would "catch it" for selling his train set.

"He'll never play with it again, and I doubt if it would even run after all these years," she said.

Down the steep stairs went Fran with the train set in her arms and out the door. I have always told her to lock the car doors as soon as she has unloaded the antiques we've bought and paid for, lest some jealous family member drive up and try to get the antiques back. No one ever tried to get into our car to do this, but believe me, several times in my lifetime they have appeared at the aunt's or mother's house just as we had everything piled on the floor that was to be sold. A frantic niece or daughter would rush in and claim all that I had bought. Or else the phone would ring and a relation would learn that antiques were being sold, and immediately appear on the scene to queer the deal.

Back to the Sanders' attic: Mrs. Sanders said there was more she wanted to sell packed in boxes, but not just then. It was getting late and Mr. Sanders would soon be home from his Elk's Club. With this I reluctantly left the attic, where I could have spent a day and still not have seen everything. There were dozens of flapper dresses, Mrs. Sanders said, put away in boxes. She especially liked to dance in her beaded one. Beaded dresses, I knew, sold for $200 each, and the ordinary flapper dress for $40 or $50. Leaving them there in the attic to go to the junkman someday made me feel like becoming insistent, but I felt I better not. Mrs. Sanders might get her dander up.

When everything had been paid for and we were about to say good-bye, in walked Mr. Sanders. Fran and I were introduced and he was told we were antique dealers from Dixon who had come to look at some dishes. Mrs. Sanders kept quiet about the other things we'd bought. Mr. Sanders then surprised me by asking if we bought old clocks. I told him yes, that I had bought several old clocks in my day.

"Well, then, follow me downtown to my store building and I'll show you some I have for sale."

When we got into Sanders' building and up to the second floor, he unlocked a door that led to some steps to the attic. There on the floor and on rickety old tables were at least 20 fine old walnut calendar clocks, triple-decker clocks with scenes in the center, and a clock with a carved eagle on the top. There were stately-looking pressed-back oak kitchen clocks, and iron clocks. Mr. Sanders asked me, "What do you think of my collection? I quit fooling around with them 20 years ago. Are you interested in buying them?"

I said, "Sure, I'll buy them if the price is right."

"What about giving me $1,000 for them?"

I pretended to be adding up in my head and

deciding whether they were worth this much, and then I looked at each one again, full well knowing that just one clock in the collection was worth close to $2,000. He didn't know which one it was, and I wasn't about to tell him, but it was a rare Seth Thomas Fashion Clock that stood over on a far table, dark and forbidding, but oh, so high priced in that year of 1981. I wasn't a clock man any more than Mr. Sanders was, but I knew it could be worth $2,500. I hesitatingly agreed to his price of $1,000, because how in hell can you cut a man down who is practically handing his clocks to you free?

We managed to haul all the clocks down that straight-up-and-down stairs without breaking our necks. The triple-deckers were almost three feet tall, so you can see with just one stumble it would have been all over for both me and the clock. The iron clocks weighed a ton, but when a big profit is being made an item somehow doesn't feel so heavy. Excitement of the kill had my vibes up and a 75-pound clock felt like a 20-pound clock.

With the last clock loaded, Mr. Sanders thanked me. I told him I was going to drive back to the house before I left town to say good-bye to his wife. He seemed to like a gent that was considerate and told me to stop again. He had more things to sell.

When I drove up to bid Mrs. Sanders good-bye and thank her for calling me, she, too, told me she'd call me again as soon as the weather cooled off so we could look through the attic in comfort. She recalled at least one of her mother's dolls being in a hump-backed trunk. That's all I needed to hear, and I took my leave, not overdoing a good thing by asking her a lot of questions.

When I got home and started to look at the orange engine on the Lionel train set, I called a friend who belonged to a train club and asked him to look up the number on the engine and the seven cars. He quickly looked it up in his train price guide, which I knew he had. I had sold cheaper trains to him before.

"The engine sells for $1,000, plus $50 for the box," he said, "and the cars retail for about $80 each." I nearly fell over. I never expected a small-size 1920's Lionel to sell for that much.

"I'll tell you who will buy your set, Dan," said my friend. "Here's his address and phone number. He is the president of the Train Collector's Clubs in America, and he lives in Boston."

I called up this president and he told me within minutes that if the set was mint that he would pay me $1,200 for it. Here I had quibbled that $100 was too high because it wasn't standard gauge, when it turned out to be one of the rarer sets Lionel made in the mid-20's.

When my customer received the set, he called and told me there was a scratch on the engine that apparently I did not see. If I would adjust the price down to $1,000 he'd keep the set. It didn't take me long to tell the president of the Train Clubs that I'd refund his $200.

I waited for the call the Sanders promised to make all through the fall, and I then decided to phone and ask about the dolls. Mrs. Sanders told me, "I sold everything in the attic to our vacuum salesman. He said he was a collector and not a dealer and would put everything he bought in his collection.''

I knew this ''vacuum'' dealer in antiques. He was broke and empty-handed in 1960 and by the time 1986 had rolled around he had spent a fortune on his house and had a van that set him back $20,000, all paid for. The ''vacuum'' business had made him a rich man because he was a professional third-story man as well.

The whole deal, once all was sold, made me over $2,500 clear, and all because Nate was too lazy to go answer the lady's letter. He was never told what I bought that day.

The way many times to make Easy Money is to go on all calls and follow up on all letters you receive. You never know what may be in the attic or basement or house-proper. Getting a foot in the door usually pays off in one way or another.

16

HAULING
OUT THE LOOT
IN WOODSTOCK

Some years ago I was interviewed for the Rockford MORNING STAR regarding my antique business. It seems one of the editors had noted the humor I put in my ads and sent the interviewer. I never in my wildest dreams had imagined that one of the editors would get a belly laugh over my ads spoofing rug buyers and decoy buyers.

The article when it appeared with pictures in a Sunday edition ran a half a page. I was soon distracted from having the big-head over this by the details of my business.

However, shortly after the article ran, I received a letter in which the writer asked if I would be interested in buying some Oriental rugs. She told me she had seen my interview in the paper, and so thought I might like them.

I called the letter-writer and asked her how many rugs, and she said ten.

"They are all old and have never been walked on because my sister who passed away last year never walked on them, and there were no children." I got even more excited as I chatted with this lady and asked how large the rugs were.

I was told the largest rug had been taken by a family member, but the rest were five and six-foot size.

Sometimes a six-foot rug can be more valuable than a room-size rug if it is the right kind. A six-foot Eagle Kazak can sell easily for $5,000, while a 9 x 12 Sarouk is lucky to bring $2,500.

I could not wait to get to the house in Woodstock, Ill. I made the appointment and was off and running for what I hoped was the biggest killing of my life.

The house that Fran pulled up in front of was pre-Civil War. When I knocked on the door, a maid answered. I asked if my wife could come in as well. Fran and I were seated on a large, well-upholstered 1840 Empire sofa. I noticed as I waited that, from plaques on the wall, this lady had been voted Woman of the Year in the town for several years. I got a bit shaky as I saw this, because I knew I wouldn't be dealing with just an ordinary lady but a brilliant one.

When she finally emerged from a side room I looked at a lady with a lot of class although she had to be in her 70's. She stood in front of me, and as we talked I was reminded of my school teachers. I asked her if she had ever taught school, and she answered that that was what she did all her life. She added that her husband was a doctor when they married, but shortly afterward he had contracted staph disease and died. She had no children, and then decided to teach school.

The rugs had belonged to her sister, but the sister had died the year before. The rugs were at the sister's house eight blocks up the street.

"I'd sure like to see them if I may," I said.

"I'll call Mr. Bush who helps around the yard and takes care of the rose garden, and ask him to drive you up. I will meet you there shortly."

While in the car Bush told us that when the sister died it was found she had bequeathed her 63 farms to Woodstock charity. Instead of having an auction sale of the household goods, it was advertised that they would be sold privately. Those who wanted to buy something in the beautiful ten-room house would tell him how much they'd give, and he would relay the bid to the schoolteacher, and she'd either approve or disapprove of the offer. In about a day the house was empty. It was the biggest sale held recently in Woodstock, and most of it was done over the phone, as the word had spread fast around the neighborhood that you could buy things at your own price.

We finally got to the house and were let in. Scattered over the living room floor were ten mint high-grade rugs. It was obvious that the family could afford the best. I could see a six-foot Kashan lying there which was the best. It was antique and worth around $3,000.

When my school-teacher friend arrived, she and

Bush started to ask me the value of various pieces of furniture that had been held back from the give-away sale. They were all important small pieces, and when I told them within a few dollars what each would retail for, they would nod their heads and whisper something to each other. When I got done appraising the furniture they asked me if I'd buy it for that price. I told them that I buy at 70% of my appraisal, and explained it was retail prices I was quoting them, not wholesale.

"I have to make money on what I buy or I couldn't stay in business," I said.

Both looked at each other and Bush told Mrs. Quinbey that the furniture should be sold to me. With this statement I found I had bought five pieces of high-priced furniture that I needed like a hole in the head. I knew they were trying me out to see if I knew my antique rug business as well. They had had a local dealer appraise all the furniture that I was asked about, and I'd hit his prices close to right on the head. This gave them confidence in me that I knew the rug business just as well.

At this point I arranged the rugs all in a row with some shorter and some larger. I started at the left end of the row and by kicking the end over I could tell by its weave what it was worth. The tighter the weave the higher priced an Oriental rug usually is. I just went down the whole line with remarks such as, "This one is shorter than the one I paid you $175 for, so I'll give you $150," and "This one is longer than the last, so I'll give you $300," all the way to the end of the line. The total came to $3,100, and I prayed for the first time in a long time, praying they'd accept my offer.

There was a hurried conference, but Bush and Mrs. Quinbey didn't hem and haw. They told me, "You were fair on your appraisal of the furniture, so go ahead and take the rugs."

I paid the $3,100 plus the money for the break-even furniture. Fran and Bush loaded my wagon as I visited with Mrs. Quinbey. She asked me to come back up to the house where she had a few other family things she wanted me to look at.

Our from a kitchen cupboard came a pink Mt. Washington cameo bride's basket all full of junk that was dirty, but the basket was so beautiful with all the four legs on the silver plated holder being cherubs. This was at least a $1,000 piece made in New Bedford, Mass. Mrs. Q. went up to the attic and came down with about 20 bundles of coin sil-verware that bore the names of important silver-smiths of the 1840's. I bought this lot along with the cameo at a fair price but not overly much. It was a deal that stood to make at least $1,000.

Mrs. Quinbey had more beautiful walnut fur-niture in the small barn behind her house, but I couldn't load any more in my wagon. I told her I'd come and get it the next day.

I then picked up a Dickensware pitcher off her shelf and bought that, too. She didn't care for it, so practically gave it to me.

When it was over and I got the throw rugs home, I ended up asking $9,000 for them. A rug dealer from Chicago came back three times to try to cut me down. He got down on his knees and sobbed that he would lose money at that price. It finally ended up with getting $6,000 for the rugs and a hefty profit on the New Bedford pink cameo bride's basket. The coin silver was sold in a big auction with knowledgeable buyers present, and it made good money.

When I called to go back the next day to pick up the beautiful walnut parlor sets and bedroom sets, Mrs. Quinbey told me she had called her niece in California and SHE wanted the furniture and would come and get it in a few months.

Just one day was all it took to lose a good deal. Strike while the iron is hot if you want to get something bought and make Easy Money.

Remember once again, if you can buy something, buy it! Don't wait an hour, let alone a day! Nieces and nephews are thicker than flies and they can seem to sense when a family piece is about to be sold.

17

ANTIQUE
RESTORATION
STUDIOS

"Arabic Art Studios" or "Cave of the Winds Art Studios" may sound like places where painting is done, but behind the sign may be another professional restorer of broken dolls, rare porcelain and scenic R. S. Prussia, as well as run-of-the-mill cracked and broken art objects. Some do excellent repairs and just as many do lousy work that shows up like a big wart on the nose.

The repair people that run their ads in all the trade papers saying they will guarantee invisible repairs are the restoration outfits to go to if you break Grandma's antique. Then should you someday want to sell it to some dealer, he will not be able to detect the repair even with his ultraviolet light! There is a cheap ultra-violet light bulb on the market for a couple of dollars that will sometimes reveal clearly the repair work in a repaired piece of china or porcelain or a doll head, if held underneath it. But it will not reveal the invisible work done by the top restoration shops.

There are literally scores of these shops working constantly to make big money for the people that mail in valuable-when-mended art objects. These objects exhibit large cracks and big chips. Doll heads have pieces out of their cheeks.

But one problem in mailing items to these miracle workers is that you are put on a waiting list, and it may be a year before you get your antique back. Another problem is a possibly exorbitant fee. Some shops charge a nominal fee, while others may try to get several hundred dollars per object for repairing. This can involve much bargaining. You better be ready to get cash and drive several hundred miles to retrieve your merchandise. A high fee and high-powered advertising do not guarantee good repairs. Why do these shops have to advertise so much? It is because word-of-mouth advertising has not helped them.

Another problem is inferior workmanship. I do not like the way some so-called art restoration studios repair bisque doll heads. The soft textured and pink bisque may come back red as a beet. The restorer is experimenting on your doll and does not have enough knowledge to do the job right. By no means send your doll to what may be a fly-by-night advertiser in a trade paper. Ask someone in the doll profession who is the best qualified to repair your doll.

A final disadvantage of repair shops is that they

all want their money in advance. If you are disatis-
fied with their work, you are out of luck.

If you are having an object repaired, the best
plan is to ask among dealers as to who does a good
repair job.

Dealing in invisibly repaired antiques is a big
business today. There are dealers who follow sales
of the most expensive china from state to state hoping that a rare piece of cracked scenic R. S. Prussia
will be auctioned off in an estate sale. Such a bowl
when perfect could easily sell for $5,000 to $10,000,
but when broken will go for only $100 or so. The
same applies to a broken Meissen statue worth
$5,000 and up if perfect but with pieces missing
from its fingers and toes worth only a fraction of
that. The buyer is always one of the men or women
who knows where to get it repaired perfectly and
who will then sell it at retail to some unsuspecting
customer. If they pull this caper off only eight or
ten times a year, they may make from $2,000 to
$5,000 each time, adding up to a tidy annual profit
of $20,000 to $25,000.

The professional repair artists can even fuse
cracked Tiffany and Steuben (signed) art glass so
you cannot detect where the crack was. They can
take a hanging glass shade with a crack and fuse
it so you cannot detect the crack.

Some years ago I got the idea that I wanted to
become a restoration expert, so I attended a repair
seminar in Chicago. The teacher told us all about
what the problems were, and then proceeded to
break a small rare scenic tapestry toothpick holder
into around 15 pieces. There they all lay where we

could get a good look at them.

The teacher took them out to the back room, and while we watched his work, he put the shards all together, worked some more magic on them, and then put them into a small kiln he carried with him.

When the three-inch holder was removed from the kiln, it was intact. Not one crack showed, and would never show, he told us, even under ultra-violet light.

I learned a valuable lesson from this, and that was to be careful when buying antiques.

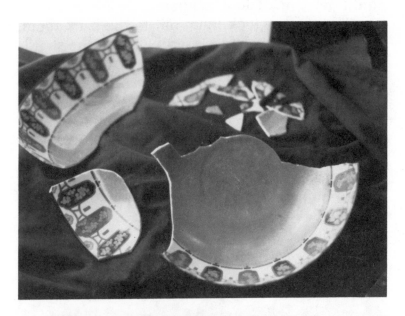

Before and after expert restoration.

18

HOW TO BECOME
A PROFESSIONAL
LIAR

Back in 1962 or '63 I got into the Oriental rug business. I didn't know a hell of a lot about it at that time. All I knew was, if an heir swore up and down the rug was a true Oriental, I'd buy it. At that time the going rate for a 9 x 12 was about $50 for Chinese to $175 high for Persian. It seemed that people wanted to get rid of them and put down wall-to-wall carpeting.

I'd wait until I had bought four or five carpets and half a dozen throw rugs, and then I'd call a man in Syracuse, N.Y., Levi Jerusalem. I had seen his ads in the magazine "Antiques" offering rugs for sale for years before I wrote him a letter asking if he would be interested in buying rugs I had purchased in my area and had no outlet for. I was told to send them in cardboard tubes that would be furnished me, and I would be contacted about what price Mr. Jerusalem could pay. At first I could never get ahold of Mr. Jerusalem himself, but when his men told him what a good Midwest source I had become for estate auction rugs, I was finally able to speak to him. The conversation was short and sweet.

"We like the rugs you have been sending us, Mr. Shiaras, and can use all that you can buy. When your shipment comes in, I will talk with you personally, or one of my men will contact you. We will offer you our top bid and if you accept, a check will be sent out to you immediately. If you feel our offer isn't up to your expectations, then the rugs will be returned at our expense."

With this he turned me over to one of his buyers and we discussed a recent shipment that had arrived by railway freight.

In those days I would be paid around $400 or $450 for a 9 x 12 rug that I had paid $50 for, buying the rugs not only at estate sales but through ads I placed in newspapers of surrounding towns. I made darn good money through my New York connection. This relationship went on until 1967, when the first Persian Oriental rug buyers started to immigrate from Persia to this area. Chicago was the stamping grounds of the Kermenian brothers, who were no sooner on American soil than they began searching high and low for rugs. Somehow they had heard about me. When they learned that I had to ship rugs to Syracuse, New York, and take whatever I could get, one of them said, "No, No, Mr. Shiaras, don't do that! Let my brother and me come out and see your rugs the next time you find some, and I promise

we will pay far more than this buyer in New York.
Here is our card!''

This meeting started an eight-year-long business
relationship. As soon as I'd get two or three good-
quality Sarouk carpets, I'd be on the phone to the
brothers' new office in downtown Chicago.

''Sure we come look,'' I'd hear one of them say.
''How about tonight? Have you got lights?''

I assured them I had lights in my 60 by 110-foot
warehouse. Right on the dot of the time arranged
one or two of the brothers would pull into my yard
and give me a honk. He didn't want to tangle with
the German shepherd I kept on the premises. I'd
call the dog off and soon we'd be in the warehouse
and my Iranian buyer would be dropping to his
knees feeling every part of the rugs for worn spots.
He then would get his flashlight out and examine
the rugs once more for pet spots.

If I had learned one thing from Mr. Jerusalem,
it was never to send him a rug with pet stains. He
told me he could not remove them and to stay away
from such rugs even if rare.

Sol Kermenian would go from one rug to
another, until all the Sarouks—three of them in the
incident I am recalling plus a Kerman throw rug—
had been thoroughly examined. Then he would say,
''Mr. Shiaras, your rugs are O.K., but they are worn
in places. See here where this rug is worn?''

As hard as I looked, I could see no wear. This
was just a ploy to get me to drop my asking price.
But Sol was not dealing with a green-horn. I told
him for all room-sized Sarouks I wanted $700 each

and for the Kerman throw rugs of good age and quality, $250.

Sol acted like I'd stabbed him in the back.

"What do you want me to do, take the rugs back to Chicago and lose money? Please, Mr. Shiaras, accept my offer of $1,500 for all the rugs! I will be paying you more than I have ever paid before for Sarouks and Kermans! What do you say, Mr. Shiaras? You are a rich man, and I am just new in this country. Please give me a break, and I will buy all your rugs from now on."

I didn't know if $1,000 profit was enough on the rugs, so I pretended to figure out costs on a piece of paper. I then would come back at Sol with, "$1,600 is the very best I can do, and I'm only selling them to you so cheap because you had to drive out here all the way from Chicago."

"Can't you make it $1,550, Mr. Shiaras? I then might take a big chance and buy them."

I'd figure once more on my pad to try to convince this Persian rug thief that I indeed was selling on a close margin. After I'd finished figuring it all out in a great act, I'd sell them at $1,500, crying that I was losing money because I had to locate them with ads in all the towns within 50 miles of Dixon.

"Do you know what my ads to buy rugs run me? $500 a month, that's what they cost!" In truth they had probably been just over a hundred. I was already learning to become a professional Oriental-rug liar like the Persians.

Sol would fold up the rugs and then with the cord he always carried, tie them so fast and securely that I became jealous of his professionalism. Some day I'm going to learn how to fold up a rug and tie it like Sol did. He lifted each of the heavy rugs to his backed-up car and thanked me, telling me to call him again when I found rugs.

Sol would hardly be back in Chicago before he would be calling me again to ask if I had found any. On the days that he did not call, his brother would call.

Soon I was lucky and got two calls in a row from home-owners who were selling out and moving to Florida. Each had seen my ads in the Rockford paper, and since these ran constantly in the wanted-to-buy section, I was the first one each thought of.

When the first caller told me she had 16 Oriental rugs to sell, Fran and I drove to a U-haul depot and hooked on a good-sized one. I also bought a heavy-duty lock to be sure once I got the rugs inside the U-haul, no one was going to change his mind.

When Fran and I and a student of mine brought along to help move the rugs were let into the house and stared at rare Kerman after rare mint Kerman beneath each bedstead, we almost keeled over. In the living room was a 24-foot palace Canton Chinese rug from the 19th Century. Under each table were rare 3 x 5 and 3 x 6 Shiraz throw rugs, which I knew immediately were worth $1,000 to $1,200 each, because they were antique and mint.

The Kermans under the beds were 1910 and worth $4,000 minimum apiece, while the Canton would easily sell for $5,000.

The lady of the house was the only one there,

and I wondered why there weren't more relatives or a husband on hand to queer our deal. We went from room to room, and when I asked her what she wanted for the 9 x 12 and 9 x 15 rare Kermans, she said $2,000. Then I asked her about the palace-size electric-blue Canton.

"There is a little tear on a corner, Mr. Shiaras, so I will sell it for $1,000." So it went all through the house until all 17 mint old Oriental rugs were accounted for.

"I think you are a good business woman, Mrs. Perry," I said, "I will not quarrel with your prices. Here is your money. Now, Ed, let's get these loaded because I have some more rugs to look at while I'm in Rockford."

The poor kid and Fran carried all those heavy rugs out. We didn't bother folding them up like my Persian friends did. We had to get out fast and get away before someone might pull up to the drive and convince Mrs. Perry of Perry Construction Co. that she had sold the rugs 'way too cheap. With a change of mind, a deal can be cancelled and a fast call made to the cops of the precinct if you should protest.

When the big 24-foot palace Canton was finally dragged out the door and thrown unceremoniously on top of the pile already in the U-haul, I quickly locked the door and turned the key.

Now let someone try to queer this deal, I thought. You have to see what you're going to queer before you can throw a bolt into the works. Before I left I walked up to Mrs. Perry and asked her how she decided on the prices she had asked. I just had to know. I had paid her $16,170 for all the rugs.

She told me the most unbelievable story I had ever heard. She said seven or eight years before, her insurance man went through the house and appraised both furniture and rugs. He wrote down what he thought the rugs were valued at, and this was the list she took her prices from. It was obvious that the insurance man had known nothing as to the rugs' value, and I doubled my investment in them, dealing this time with an Oriental rug firm on Michigan Avenue in Chicago. This deal made enough money to run ads in the Rockford paper for 100 years, with some left over.

Ed, my helper, was dead tired when we got back home and got unloaded.

"Today was the fastest I've moved in my life," Ed said. I could not lift at this time because of a head-on car crash that left me severely disabled.

When I called the next day to the second house to say I'd be up to buy their rugs, just as there is frequently, there was a change of mind.

"A niece and her husband from out of town stopped by, and seeing all the beautiful rugs, asked if they could buy them, so we agreed that they could. Thank you for calling, Mr. Shiaras."

This interference at the last moment by relatives stepping into my deal has made a nervous wreck out of me when it comes to house calls. Just when I'm ready to pay for a fine, room-sized Oriental that will double its money, the phone will invariably ring. When the lady of the house answers, she says, "I have an antique dealer over here, Dear, and I'm selling him the rug that I have rolled up in the basement. You say don't sell it until you get over here? Alright, I'll wait."

I just put my money back in my billfold, because I know from experience that the niece will queer the deal in one way or another. One time, one came rushing in telling Aunt that the rug was hers!

"Remember a long time ago when you promised it to me? I know it's worth $10,000 in Chicago."

There I was offering $500 for it, and the niece came out with the $10,000 figure, when in reality the rug would bring no more than $1,000. In this case I was told in no uncertain terms by the niece to get out because all the glass and china and the rug were to be hers when Aunt died.

I had another rug buyer who had come over from Tehran, where his brother had owned a valuable rug mall, but could no longer do business profitably after Komeini took over. No matter what rugs you bought, it seemed some Persian could smell them 100 miles away. The calls at the last of my intense hunt for rugs started coming in from five or six dealers in Chicago and some from Minneapolis who had heard that I dealt in good rugs, and probably that I sold them considerably under what they were worth. I will never know if they were underpriced, because the Persian rug dealers talk their own language in front of you when two come to buy.

The rugs they'd buy from me would probably end up in 5th Avenue New York shops and in highrise apartment suites. Oriental rugs were also much in demand from German buyers. If you ever visited a home in Germany, you would see wall to wall Oriental carpets. They also use them for table covers and wall hangings. They had to be mint. Worn rugs usually ended up in Italy, because the Italians didn't have the money to buy good rugs. But they had a taste for them and were satisfied with buying worn rugs that if perfect would have sold for large sums of money.

If you want to watch the professional rug buyers in action, you can go to Dunning's, where one man controls the entire group of 20 Iranian rug buyers, and he is the one that does all the buying. After the sale they take the rugs out and another auction takes place with each individual paying the rest evenly what he would have paid in Dunning's. In other words, by letting one man do the bidding, they have kept the price down for themselves.

Even to this day I am not sure whether I sold the Persians my rugs too high or too low. They are a very secretive nationality that will not divulge one trick of the trade to a non-Persian. You can't get ahead of a race of people who when children of eight or nine tied with their nimble fingers a million tight knots in a rug.

19

MY ANTIQUE STUDENT
HITS THE
JACKPOT

In the fall of 1989 I read of a sale to be held just north or Oregon, Illinois, only 20 miles away, that was advertised as offering two primitive oil paintings. They depicted a man and a woman and were painted by an itinerant artist.

This ad piqued my interest, as it was listed in two national antique publications. To spend so much money on advertising meant this might be a worthwhile sale. There were also to be three auctioneers.

When Fran and I drove up to the sale site, we found it was being held at a home on the Rock River that was lived in only in summer. It had been kind of a mystery house to us as we had driven by it and seen the unlit windows and the house up on a hill almost hidden by trees and weeds.

As we walked through the yard, all we saw at first were a lot of nearly new appliances, furniture, and dishes. The yard was at least 75 by 200 feet and jammed. When I wondered out loud where all this new junk had come from, someone told me that it had all come out of the house and basement and the large garage. I estimated it would take the three auctioneers three or four hours to sell it.

I then inquired where the "good stuff" was, and was told that the fine china, glass, and the primitive paintings were all in the basement. The first section that we entered contained the dishes, which turned out to be sets that had been purchased over the past 30 years and were of no interest to an antique dealer. It was when we moved into another room in the basement that I almost had "a big one." The room was filled with watercolors, framed and unframed, most of a recent origin. But what riveted my eyes on the wall facing me were the two great primitive portraits. One showed a stern-looking old lady in a bonnet, and the other, a man writing with a quill pen. I could easily see they were from the 1810-1830 period.

The portraits were not signed, so I figured that this artist, like so many itinerant artists of that day, had simply painted the two subjects, received payment, and went on his way.

I noticed a six-inch tear across the center of the lady's portrait, but I knew it could be repaired so it would never show.

At that moment in walked a man and his lady backer. It was my former student, whom I had taught all I knew about antiques over a period of eight years, and then he had gone on to learn all there was to know about American folk art from one of the best authorities in the Mid-west. I immediately knew that with all the money his lady backer represented, I did not stand a chance of buying the paintings. You cannot beat the combination of money and knowledge. All you ever get is overpaying and being stuck with something that you will lose your shirt over when trying to sell it.

I briefly discussed the paintings with my former student and then motioned Fran to quit visiting and leave. As I passed my friend, I turned back and told him he'd have to pay $10,000 to buy the paintings. I had no sooner said this than a man brushed by me in a hurry to depart who said, ''He's going to have to pay a hell of a lot more than that.''

The three auctioneers started this sale outdoors at 11 a.m. and were still on the first hayrack at 12:30 when we departed the scene.

That evening I got a call from my excited former student, who told me he had bought the paintings. He said he paid $9,200 for the man and only $8,000 for the lady because of the rip. Then he told me something that nearly floored me. He said he'd been at the scene the day before the sale and had looked on the backs of the paintings for a signature, and down in the lower corner of each painting on the stretcher in small letters was the signature of the greatest primitive artist of all time, Ammi Phillips, and the date, Sept. 15, 1816!

I, like my friend, had thought that all Ammi Phillips paintings had been accounted for and either hung in museums or in very wealthy homes. My student said he had started sweating from the minute he saw the signatures up until the minute the second portrait was sold to him, with the opposing bidder being the second young man who had told me, "He'll have to pay a lot more than $10,000 for them." That fellow, as it turned out, is a collector of more modern art, but seeing the primitive paintings were done so well, he thought he'd try and buy them. He is said to have money up to his armpits, so why he didn't bid higher was a mystery. Later he told me he did not know they were signed.

My former student was so excited as he talked that he nearly burned up the phone. He told me, "Dan do you know Ammi Phillips paintings could easily sell at Sotheby's in New York for $500,000? Now I'm going to be able to live like you do, buy anything, and do anything I want. This is the chance I've been waiting for."

After he hung up, I began to wonder, how did two great paintings like this hang in this home all these years without anyone turning them around to see if they were signed? Or did the owners know, but just fail to tell the heirs?

Ten days later I saw my student again at a sale. He pulled out photos he'd taken of both the paintings and other paintings by Ammi Phillips. Sure enough, they were identical in style. Then he showed me a photo of the signatures he'd found in tiny letter on the backs, and these, too, were identical to the Ammi Phillips signature that was in the primitive painting book he owned.

He had taken the damaged painting to Chicago and had it repaired, and then drove immediately to Sotheby's to consign both paintings for the next primitive painting and folk art sale in March. The pre-sale estimate was $250,000.

They could blow the roof off the primitive art record for a pair of Ammi Phillips works, he was told, and sell for as much as $500,000.

I will always blame the greenhorn auctioneers for not examining the paintings more closely. Had they seen the signatures and advertised these works for what they were, the entire folk art community from Coast to Coast would have descended on what should have been a heavily guarded hall, not a basement.

Salegoers were shocked when the paintings sold for $18,000, I was told. What would have been their reaction if two really big-time gallery buyers were there bidding against one another?

We will not know until later this year how much the pair of paintings will bring. I can hardly wait to see my former student driving a new Mercedes Benz.

The Ammi Phillips oil on canvas signed and dated portraits discussed in this chapter.

My former antique student, lucky buyer of the portraits, being paid a visit by Illinois Gov. James Thompson, who enjoys antiques.

20

"NOTHING TO BE
REMOVED UNTIL
SETTLED FOR"

I subscribe to a weekly paper that carries Byron, Illinois, news and also that of surrounding communities. What is of interest to me is that it carries almost all the antique sales listed in other papers. Many times heirs to an estate do not want to spend much money in advertising, so some of these sale notices get no further than this weekly, and I may be the only major dealer who reads them.

The auctioneer at many of these sales is Sid Tansie, whom I first knew as a livestock auctioneer with his dad. At that time I was a combination antique picker and bonded and licensed livestock dealer.

How I hated the name picker! Many times I'd be in a shop and be introduced by the dealer to another dealer as "one of my pickers." Once I was introduced as "my best picker" and for the first time I felt proud of being a lowly picker instead of the operator of a genuine antique shop.

While I was honing up to become a national mail order dealer, Sid Tansie kept selling everything from billy goats to cattle. Eventually Old Man Tansie sold the sale barn and Sid went into real estate. Along with this came the call many times to sell the contents of a house. Those were the sales that you could depend on making you some serious money. But the way Sid would word his ads would keep the hawks away, because what was signed cut glass and worth good money, he didn't advertise as cut glass, let alone signed. "Lots of good, pressed glass," he would say. He'd have all kinds of strange names for signed art glass, calling beautiful, shimmering Tiffany "carnival glass." This is where I'd made Easy Money. He had a long way to go to be an antique auctioneer.

One day as I was reading the TEMPO, I read that an estate auction was to be held only seven miles from my home at the Polo, Illinois Colliseum. In big letters at the top, the bill read, "100 pieces of beautiful purple glass." There were more interesting antiques, but the purple glass intrigued me. Was it possible that the deceased had collected rare 1890 purple Croesus pressed glass decorated with gold?

As usual we arrived about ten minutes into the sale and had no way to examine the purple glass that was on center tables surrounded by tables of junk and a crowd of bidders. The junk, of course, was all sold first, and still none would move and lose their spot so I could examine the purple glass on the back of the tables. It was Croesus, I felt sure. The only thing that worried me was whether it was perfect.

Tansie by this time had hundreds of estate sales to look back upon. He never failed to tell bidders, "You better love what you buy, because it's yours. Don't send it back. If we took back every chip, pimple, and flake, I'd be selling this sale until dark."

So if you spent $400 on a berry bowl and six individual dishes, and one was cracked, you had no recourse, even though the set was ruined as far as selling at a profit.

I saw Lacy Pants from Shannon over to the right, and to the left against a wall sat Old Man Otis, both experts on glass and you-name-it. I figured if I ever outdistanced those two, it would be a miracle.

The bidding began on the beautiful purple Croesus. Tansie told the crowd absolutely nothing about it. He just said he would now sell the "purple glass."

In succession I bought a berry set, a water pitcher and six tumblers. Then I bought the table set of a sugar, creamer, covered butter, and a spooner for the low price of $325. This I could not understand. My two arch rivals were watching and not bidding. When it was over I had spent $1,600.

Only then could Fran go back to the front row of tables and pack what I had bought. When she was through she came over to me and said she didn't think the Croesus looked like old 1890 Croesus, but like repro Croesus.

I walked quickly over to the executor of the estate and asked him if he knew when his mother and father acquired it. He told me it was bought new from Marshal Field's about 40 years before, and he had told Tansie that before the sale.

"Would you let me return it?" I asked. "I can't sell new glass of any kind."

"It's not new. I just told you, didn't I, that its almost 40 years old!"

"It's supposed to be 100 years old to be saleable, and not 40 years. It sounds to me like Tansie purposely didn't tell the crowd the age of this glass, and let them think it was old, so he could get more commission."

"Well, if you want to see Tansie after the sale and see what he says, that's OK with me."

I told Fran to pick out a pitcher and take it out to the car where we had a chipped purple Croesus pitcher, and compare the two. There was no comparison between the old and the new. The gold on the old was painted straight and true, whereas the gold work on the 40-year-old pitcher was wavering. I threw up my hands in disgust.

Now I knew why Lacy Pants and Otis had not bid against me. I walked over to the executor again, and told him I stood to lose a lot of money on the glass and had been led to believe it was old and not modern. He told me he had nothing to do with it and I would have to see Tansie after the sale.

I knew about how that Hitler would react. He had a bad temper and would threaten to call the cops.

I walked around with Fran, thinking and talking about what in hell to do. $1,600 was at stake in this mess I had got myself into because we had gotten to the sale too late to examine the Croesus.

Then I remembered that at the bottom of the sale bill Tansie had put, "Nothing to be removed until settled for!"

A bright light went on in my head. I told Fran that if we didn't pay for the repro glass, then we couldn't take it out of the hall. I told Fran, "Push all the boxes full of Tansie's sick repro glass under the clerk's table and tell her what's there. Tell her we are short of money and can't pay for it. I'll be parked out in front headed towards Grand Detour when you come out and we'll make a break for it.

We got home, which was seven miles, and I kept a nervous lookout for Tansie to drive up and raise some hell, but he didn't show or call. I decided at 8 p.m. to go across to the Landmark to have a drink or two to relax my nerves, and was only into my first drink when I was paged to come to the phone.

The voice on the other end of the line came from an angry, loud, and drunk-sounding Tansie. He shouted for me to get the hell up to his office in the morning and pay for what I bought.

"You got me stuck with your Croesus," he screamed, "and you'd better pay for it or else. I mean it, Shiaras!"

I replied, "Your sale bill says I don't have to pay for it unless I haul it out!"

Tansie slammed the receiver in my ear, and this was the end of my going to his auctions for two years.

Then one day when I read in the paper that he was holding a very juicy two-day sale, again in Byron, I called him and asked if it would be alright for me to come.

"It's been a long time since I've gone to your auctions, and I'd like to come to the one you're having Saturday and Sunday."

"OK, Dan, but you're going to have to pay the clerk as we go."

Fran and I were there, carrying $3,000 in small bills to keep feeding the clerk for everything as I bought it all day. With my first purchase, Tansie waved me to keep my money in my pocket.

This was the best thing that could have happened to Tansie and me, because I made his sale a real sale instead of a steal by a bunch of cheap flea market dealers. I made them pay if they got an antique away from me, which was very few. This high bidding brought Tansie more and more commissions. It has been good between us now for a long time, and I intend to keep it that way.

"A Fast Exit"

Note: Green croesus sells for 50% less than purple.

21

OPENING
AN
ANTIQUE SHOP

The first thing to do is pick a place where there is a high density of traffic from out of state, preferably on the edge of town or on a busy highway. Never build nor rent off the beaten path, unless you are in a city of 500,000 or more.

It is out-of-towners who love seeing an attractive antique sign along the road along with a neat shop, that will stop and patronize you. Most dealers like myself and collectors as well cannot resist stopping at such a place. They figure if it looks neat and clean on the outside, it will have good antiques inside.

The other reason for picking such a location is that if you have bought or built and business doesn't pan out, then you can always sell easily.

If you build a building, build a steel building

at least 60 feet long by 30 feet wide in an attractive
color with large windows facing the traffic. Make
your building light and airy. Then install adequate
heating and air conditioning so that the shop will
always stay comfortable. This is conducive to holding the customer in longer. The longer customers
look around, the better the chance that they will
see something that appeals to them.

Try to have an adequate number of show cases
on each side of the room so that your glass, china,
jewelry, and watches can be easily seen. In order
to do a good business you must keep the shop well-
stocked with quality goods. You can't sell from an
empty shelf.

Next, keep up to date through trade papers on
what antiques are selling the best at antique auctions around the country. Many trade papers not
only picture these antiques but report how much
they sold for.

I would advise the new shop owner to concentrate equally on what both ladies and men buy. Have
a good display of dolls attractively dressed on stands
in one part of the show case, because they are without doubt one of the best selling antiques. I'd go
to dealers and buy 25 or 30 and tack 25 or 30% or
more onto their prices. The reason you can mark
up a doll up to 50% is because in lots of cases it
is not the money the doll is priced at that counts,
instead it is how much she appeals to the collector.
No matter how cheap a price you put on an unat-
tractive doll, you will have a much more difficult
time trying to sell her to out-of-town buyers than
the $500-and-up doll that carries a well-known

name and is perfect. Very few times should you invest in a doll with even the smallest damage, such as a chip on the eyelid or a hairline crack on the head. Just as a piece of fine signed Tiffany art glass will sell for one or two thousand if perfect but will not sell at all when cracked, so with dolls.

Next along the show case, fine antique jewelry should be displayed. No cheap constume jewelry, but at least 30 pieces of antique gold jewelry like cameos and rings with attractive stones. These two items sell the best to women at auctions I attend. Women go crazy over rings at auctions.

Then go out and buy a good supply of quality hatpins. They can sell from $25 for the saddest-looking ones to up to $75 for the rarest. At auctions, the bidding is unbelievable once a hatpin collection has been nationally advertised. Collectors drive in from several states to get a crack at them. We who are used to seeing hat pins sell for $10 or $15 locally need to take in a red-hot hat pin sale every once in a while to wake us up to their true value.

The longer the pin's shaft, the older the pin. A shaft that is 11 or 12 inches long pre-dates 1900 in most instances. Have a nice supply on hand at all times and display them in quality hat pin holders like R. S. Prussia if you can find them. R. S. Germany and Germany will do. Hat pin holders signed Nippon sell just as high as the R. S. Germany. Hat pin holders are one of my best sellers along with hat pins and dolls, so don't fail to have an adequate supply of each.

You can watch for the doll sales in trade papers and go where they are and buy. Don't come home empty-handed because you think the prices are too high. Just buy some and tack a higher price on them. They will bring in the ladies. Ladies will come in to admire your dolls, and then perhaps settle for a lower-priced antique. Only 1% of the lady customers in your shop may buy a high-priced doll, but that will help pay your overhead.

I would then line the showcases with high, button shoes, granny glasses, several pieces of 1900's lacy white underwear and 1900's dresses.

I would carry a few dozen Royal Doulton lady figurines. They always sell high at sales, and travellers going through town who know these antiques will buy them.

In the back of your shop try to carry a nice selection of refinished oak and walnut marble-top furniture such as tables and bedroom sets. Keep all the oak you can adequately display because it sells as well as fine walnut or better. Wash stands with towel bars, three-drawer dressers with mirrors, and highboys with serpentine drawers are the best sellers.

Try to have pickers bring what they buy to your shop and pay for it. The furniture will sell for a lot more to a buyer coming through from California or Texas where the supply of oak is short and the prices are astronomical.

Have a good supply of choice hanging lamps, lit and hanging. It is not hard to sell a cranberry hobnail shade and hanging lamp for $1800 or $1900 to the advanced collector. I've bid in the last year up to $1,575 apiece for three such lamps, and they all were sold to lamp DEALERS.

Carry a nice supply of table lamps, ones like the sweetheart finger lamp, Lincoln Drape, etc.

Keep the shop well-supplied. Don't ever let it become 2/3 or half empty because that indicates to the buyer that all the goodies have been sold.

Down one side of the store, cater to the men by having a good selection of tin and cast iron toys in fine condition. Invariably the boy will come out in a man who collects toys and he will spend $400 or $500 just for a tin or cast iron Arcade toy and for many other brands. Keep a good selection of toys from cap pistols of the 1930's and 1920's steel trucks and toys copied from heavy machinery. 1920's Buddy-L toys lead the prices, often retailing for over $1,000. It is nothing to see a collection of Buddy-L fire engines sell for over $600 each. Keystone made a good steel toy and it will sell, but not like Buddy-L. Stay with a few Buddy-L 1920's toys, and you will soon be found out as the place to come and buy good toys.

If you keep some original-paint or 70% original-paint mechanical banks on hand, they won't last long. Just order some from some reliable bank dealer who advertises in a trade magazine and mark them up 30%. It is an easy way to make Easy Money.

Still banks on the rarer side also sell out fast when in nice condition. There are over 3,000 different still banks, so you won't have too hard a time buying some from a dealer.

Along your walls keep a good selection of crisp old quilts. Blue is the best seller and red is #2. Fine appliqued quilts are the very best sellers, bringing from $600 to $1,000. Don't buy washed-out old quilts or ones with holes. Stay with the mint, never-on-the-bed kinds, and you won't be able to keep up with the demand at even $300 to $400 if finely quilted and some calico thrown in. I have bought and sold a thousand and more quilts in my day and now when I picture a row of ten or 15 in my ads, all are sold the first or second day the paper is out. All ladies love fine old quilts and money is no object to out-of-staters when they see what they must have. I've sold quilts as high as $800 to dealers and they take them to states like California and sell them for a lot more.

Have some guns on hand, preferably Winchester rifles and Colt pistols, as well as Nazi regalia.

Large sulfide and swirled marbles sell easily for $150 each if about three inches in diameter for the swirled and two inches for the sulphide with its cute little animal figures inside blown into the glass, circa 1840.

Do not depend on local customers to sell to. The locals just don't seem to want to spend money with a local dealer for some reasons, and this I have never been able to figure out. Antique dealers tell me, "If I depended on local business I'd go broke in a month." It's the out-of-stater going by the shop that will stop and buy something, perhaps $1,000-worth of antiques. So always keep this in mind when deciding where to locate your shop.

It is best to locate inside town where you will have police protection. Then I would install a burglar alarm. It is the best deterrant to burglaries that

I know. Once your place has been cased and they see the burglar alarm signs, you can rest at night. Burglars will not attempt to break into a shop that carries the Kat's Eye Burglar Alarm warning seal on your door.

You must have good help who know how to sell on Saturdays and Sundays. These will be your days to go to antique estate sales to buy good quality furniture and Haviland china sets, plus anything else that is mint and attracts your eye.

Do all these things and you can't help but succeed. You have stocked the shop with almost everything a buyer might ask for.

Ca. 1890 Star of Bethlehem, $750-$850
Ca. 1880 Log Cabin, $750-$850

22

HOW TO GET ROOKED
IN SELLING
MOTHER'S HEIRLOOMS

Joel told me the story of how Fred Knight and Joel as his helper bought out a complete, important local estate from the daughter of the family. Knight had been called in because he had sold many of the antiques to the family, and they believed he had dealt fairly with them. Fred called Joel to go with him on this raiding party.

The estate included a huge collection of early pewter, Rose Medallion china, 1840 Canton china, painted Pennsylvania Dutch furniture, rosemalled trunks, 1840 flint glass, large folio prints of Currier and Ives and Inness, and quite a few ordinary antiques.

Daughter Flora knew the value of a smattering of the most expensive pieces, because she had heard her folks discuss their prices. As Fred started in on

Room 1, Flora helped him out often by remarking, "I know how much that piece is worth."

Knight responded by offering more than an item was worth on the antiques that Flora knew were valuable, and then grabbed a whole series of items that she knew nothing about for next to nothing. Fred cleaned out all the bookcases that had been transformed by Flora's father to hold their red ware that is very high priced, along with rows of mottled Galena pottery in unusual forms. Fred would bid high on one or two pieces on the shelf and then practically steal the rest by saying the remainder were not decorated the way he liked. He cleaned out 40 pieces of red ware for peanuts when they were worth at least $10,000.

He then gave the Galena pottery a good working over, aided by the fact that Flora thought it was ugly and two pieces were cracked or chipped, which Fred said knocked down the collection's worth. He bid the same for these rare Galena jugs that ran from a quart size to five gallons as he would bid on plain stoneware jugs.

"This is the best I can do for you, Flora, with all that damage," Fred said. Actually, there were 40 pieces of Galena in three cabinets with the five-gallon mottled jug on the floor. Joel said that Flora did not even hesitate at accepting Fred's bid of $30 a jug and $50 for the five-gallon of great rarity. So Fred picked up rare Galena jugs in all kinds and sizes for $1,250 when in actuality each jug was selling at all sales in the area for $200, and the biggie would sell for $400.

If there was a print that Fred figured Flora knew

the value of, he would pay more than it was worth, then "swipe" for less some winter and train scenes that were more valuable. He swiped around $6,000 worth of Currier and Ives at $150 each.

This was a night of nights for Joel, because he was learning how to go through an estate and buy at a profit. When it had all been gone over, Knight wrote out a check for $13,000 and asked Flora to hold it for a week, which Flora agreed to. Hardly anyone else alive would have gotten away with this.

Fred and Joel filled up Fred's station wagon three times that night, making four 50-mile trips to Fred's house with the loot. When it came to common junk and large pieces of oak furniture, Fred and Joel just put them on Flora's front porch, telling her they'd be back for them later. Fred never did go back to the scene of the crime for fear that after Flora looked at her folks' insurance policy on the collection he might get shot. Fred told Joel that he should clear $40,000 on the deal, and this was all because Flora had trusted Fred. Hadn't he sold her mother and father piece after piece of pewter and red ware when they were alive? Hadn't they always told her that if anything should happen to them, to call Fred to buy their collection because "he's always been fair with us"?

"Being fair" didn't mean he wasn't over-pricing all the antiques he ever sold them. They had Old Money. What was $100 more on something they liked?

My advice for people like Flora is to take their antiques to an auction gallery like Dunning's in Elgin, Ill., one of the most important auction

galleries west of Sotheby's in New York. At such a
gallery there are sophisticated and well-informed
buyers that drive in from Chicago and its suburbs
and are dying to buy early American decorated
furniture and pewter, large folios of trains leaving
the station and the rarest Currier of all showing a
grizzly bear attacking a hunter that would sell for
$5,000 to $6,000 at auctions, not for the $150 that
Fred paid.

No wonder Fred had told Joel, "We've got to
get it all out tonight because Flora might change
her mind!"

23

THE
BRASS BED
KING

During the 60's and up until 1972 the hunting down of brass beds proved to be very lucrative. One day I went to Galena, Illinois, and as I walked down the street I saw an old brass bed standing in the window of an antique shop. The tag on it surprised me. It was $395. I began to talk with the young dealers, and they promised me they'd pay me $100 for every brass bed I could find, plus a bonus of $50 if the posts were extra large with large cannon-ball caps.

They also told me that of brass beds, the majority were just brass-wrapped, with 1/16 of an inch of brass around steel posts. Only the caps and a few other parts would be solid brass.

The best way to buy a brass bed cheap, they said, was to carry a magnet with you, and when you went in a house to buy a bed, put the magnet

up against the post. "It will stick to the brass
because it is so thinly wrapped," said the cagey
young dealers, "and you can tell the seller that the
bed is only brass-painted on steel, and get it cheap.
Tell them you can still use it for parts and offer them
$10 or $20."

When I got home I decided to map out a plan
of attack to try to buy all the brass beds I could before
other local dealers got wise as to their value. I picked
Dixon, Illinois, as the center of my advertising and
made a 50-mile circle around it on a map and began
advertising within the circle, saying I'd pay $25 for
old brass beds. This was just a bit more money than
the young dealers from Galena suggested I pay, but
it made a nice round figure. One week I'd pick a
group of towns to advertise in in one direction, and
the next week I'd go in another direction.

In this manner I got my start as the Brass Bed
King of the Middle West.

The letters came pouring in. Anyone who
owned an ugly, unpolished brass-wrapped bed,
since it was usually in disuse in attic or basement,
was more than willing to sell it for $25, without my
resorting to the magnet. Some days, with Fran driving, we'd head out with six or seven letters to follow up on. Fifty percent would turn out to be
painted brass and just junk, while the other half
were brass-wrapped and worth $100 each. We'd
usually pick up about four brass-wrapped beds on
each trip. We would make a strange spectacle by the
time three or four head rails were tied on top of our
station wagon.

At times I was led into upstairs bedrooms where

no one had slept for years, and there would be a pair of single brass beds with nice straight posts and large brass caps. I've hauled beds out of crawl spaces piece by piece and out of basements with a half-foot of water in them.

Every once in awhile I would go to buy what I thought would be an ordinary brass-wrapped bed, and behold, it would be an ornate, bow-front bed with cannon-ball caps worth a minimum of $400. Bow-fronts were always solid brass and made for the rich of their day. The owner would sometimes ask if it was worth the $25 I had advertised I would pay. I'd pretend it was a bit high, but in the end I'd tell the seller I guessed I would buy it, as it would fit in with others I had. I might be able to make $10 or $15 if the right buyer came along. Any statement about a possible high profit such as $100 would mean I would have gone home empty-handed.

There was one brass-wrapped bed it was best not to buy, and that was the kind with a rounded head. We used the term "hospital beds" for them. The market was not there for that shape of bed, even if you tried to sell it for $10 or $20. They were just plain ugly.

One thing to remember in acquiring an antique brass bed is that it will cost $100 to $150 to have it polished and lacquered so the finish will stay bright. In evaluating brass beds, the bigger the posts are in diameter and the larger the caps, the more valuable the bed. In the days when I was dealing in beds, I would sell an average brass bed to the Freeling Brothers for around $125 to $150, and they would mark it up to $225 to $250. When it came to the bed with larger posts and caps, I'd sell it for $250 and they would mark it up sometimes to $450.

Once in awhile in the 60's I'd advertise 100 brass beds for sale in the "Antique Trader." I'd get the most response from the West Coast and California dealers. One time it was a Seattle, Washington, dealer who called first, and when his cashier's check for 100 beds arrived, it was for $15,000. I always tagged the head, foot, and rails with masking tape bearing corresponding numbers so that the buyer would not have to spend two or three days trying to find the right rails for 100 beds.

One time I made out an ad that included the Streator area, and the last bed that Fran and I picked up on our trip into that section was stuck up in an attic and was painted green. I tried to convince the lady seller that it would take a lot of money to remove the green paint. She tried to convince me that it looked better painted green.

"It would look nice in your house, or do you sell them?" she asked. I told her I was just trying to redo my home, and green would not do. She would not budge from the $25 I had offered in my ad, so up went a green bed on top of our wagon.

Many of the beds I would be contacted to buy as a result of my ads would be brass-painted iron beds and of no worth to me. After a few foul balls like this, I would hit a bowfront bed.

A baby's brass bed would bring more than a large, four-poster bed because they are so rare. I sold the only one I ever found to a dealer friend for $500. I suppose he jacked the price up to $600 or $700.

We learned never to buy beds with a poster

missing or even a cap missing. Chances are a match would never be located. If rails were missing it was not such a problem. They could be found at a neighborhood junk yard and made to fit by someone who did welding.

We found that one thing is a must when loading brass beds. You must remove the casters. They have a tendency not to come home with you. To sell, a brass bed must look straight and true.

One of my strangest experiences occurred when I was called to a farm about fifty miles away to look at a bed. I found it had been stored in a hay mow for a long time.

''We'll just lower it down out of the doors we use when we pull up hay and straw,'' the farmer said. When the bed appeared in the hay mow doors suspended by a rope, I almost keeled over, because it was the solid brass kind with a high, ornate headboard reminiscent of New Orleans brothels but hardly seen in the Midwest. I could hardly wait until the head and foot hit the ground to see if it was all there. A missing part on such a beautiful bed could be its undoing, because there would be no replacing its parts. They are one of a kind.

After all the parts were lowered and fitted together, I knew I had a $1,000 bed. Now came the time for me to make the decision of what to pay the farm folks for it. It had been in the family since the 19th Century, and I knew from looking at them that they weren't just born yesterday. I was even thinking that there might be a change of mind about selling the bed once it was set up and shining so brilliantly like gold in the sun. It even had some pieces of decorated porcelain on it to give it more class.

The usual questions were batted back and forth. "Well, folks, what do you want for your bed? I buy quite a few like this one, so I know about what I can pay to make $25."

Never tell a seller of a major piece of furniture or any other antique object of value that you are going to make over $25 on it, or you are going home empty-handed. The minute a seller hears that you can make $100 on something, you may as well forget it. He will tell you that if he decides to sell it, he will call you, but he never does.

"What'll you give us for it?" countered the farmer. "It wasn't eating anything up in the mow, so we don't have to sell it if your offer isn't right."

Back you come with, "I can't be the buyer and seller both. What do you want for it?" (Try never to make an offer—let the seller set his price.)

Then comes the old story from the farmer, "We don't know what brass beds like this are selling for, so you're going to have to make us an offer."

At this point the men are separated from the boys in brass bed buying. One must know within a few dollars what price the sellers have on their minds for their ancestors' Civil War-era brass bed. Fortunately, they do not see it as the best brass bed to ever come up for sale in the Midwest. All they see is a certain amount of dollar bills. Their old wooden bed is what they think is beautiful and not this brass work of art.

I stood there a moment as if thinking and seeming to count on my fingers how much I could pay without going in the hole. I couldn't offer too much and scare them off, so I came out with a preposterously low offer of $175.

Farmers who hardly see this much money all at once in a coon's age don't even bother to say "Sold." All this one said was, "Back up and let's get it loaded."

Evidently in my anxiety to be sure to buy the bed, I had bid $100 over what they expected to get. After paying them in cash, I told Fran to back the wagon up, and we loaded the best bed I was to own in my ten years of advertising every week for them. I took it home and stood it up along a row of 100 or more beds in my 110-foot long warehouse, and it stood up at least two feet higher than any other. I knew I had a bed worth $1,000 and even more to the Freeling Brothers.

One day Nick Freeling came down to buy a load of 25 brass beds for his Galena shop. His eyes nearly popped out when he saw standing before him the queen of solid, ornate brass beds, with its areas of floral porcelain. But he tried to do exactly like I do, and knocked it. After downgrading the bed for some time, he finally decided that my price of $750, reduced from my original $1,000, stood, and he better buy it before the next brass bed dealer showed up. He loaded up all his beds without putting a blanket between them, but when it came to the prize-winning bed, he carefully wrapped it up in packing quilts which he had brought along.

About six months later Nick invited me to come and see an old house he and his brother had bought in Galena and remodelled, papering it with just-right wallpaper and furnishing it with just the right period furniture. He led me into his bedroom, and laughing like a baboon he pointed to the bed I had sold him. I was not a bit jealous, because it was these two young men who had started me in the brass bed business where I made a lot of Easy Money by advertising for brass beds and not waiting for someone to come to me with one to sell.

I continued this very profitable bed business until new brass beds started taking over the market. Today old brass beds sell for half-price compared to what they brought 15 years ago. I guess the brass bed fad is over, because I hardly see any in big department stores. What was once a prestige item and went out of style, then arose to become once more a sign of affluence, has again gone out of fashion. I wonder if all those brass beds I sold will get hot and sell again in the year 2,000?

24

THE
FOOTLESS BLACKMAN
WHIRLIGIG

In the summer of 1988 I read in the Dixon paper that a nondescript sale was to be held south of Rock Falls by a schoolteacher who had entered a nursing home. I heard rumors that she'd been buying, buying, buying anything and everything that she could get her hands on for a long time, and storing the articles in the outbuildings around the farm home where she and her husband had lived for 50 years. The sale bill, however, made no mention of anything old or particularly interesting.

I told Fran that since there wasn't another Saturday sale in a wide area, we would take a quick run down to this sale and have a look. When we finally pulled into the sale area where a large crowd had gathered, I told Fran the sale might turn out to be a ''sleeper,'' because everyone we knew who was in the antique business and the collectors, too, were already looking over the heaped-high hay racks.

The first two racks we looked at were both loaded down with old hats. I have never seen this many hats, even when a division of soldiers were standing at attention. The next two racks were loaded with coats of every size and description. The teacher must have had an ''in'' with a coat manufacturer.

There were some interesting collectibles, like a large copper apple butter kettle, old-time banana crates with advertising, a dozen or so hat pins. Not too much, I thought, until I looked on one of the back tables. There I saw one of the rarest whirligigs I'd ever seen, covered with many years of grime. The 16-inch high whirligig represented a black man with a tin hat and fat body with legs that were broken off at the ankle. He was painted in bright colors. His arms were yellow and in the shape of 12-inch propellers that when you hung him from the steel loop on top of his hat to a tree limb or on a porch, would turn like propellers. As the arms turned, they chased away a bee on a wire. I guessed that this hand-made novelty dated from about 1875 and had its original paint.

Such whirligigs were carved on many farms. The older they are, the higher priced, and double or triple their ordinary price when in the form of a black person.

I knew that with a couple of experienced dealers in attendance, that trouble was afoot for me to nail this great American primitive carving.

The auctioneer finally, after four hours, got done selling six or eight hay racks full of some good and some bad collectibles and worked his way back to the comical Blackman whirligig. He started this dust-covered rarity at $1! The next bid was $5, and then $100, and $200. Finally at $210, with myself being the last bidder, I became the new owner of my fat Blackman. We drove home, and while Fran was visiting friends, I thought I had better wash off the 125 years of dirt to see how he would look. He came out almost like the day he was painted.

On close examination, though, I noticed I had taken some of the black and yellow paint off, leaving the body speckled.

"Nuts," I said to myself, "now I've ruined it some more. It was bad enough that his feet were gone, leaving splintered-looking ankles."

About this time I received a call from a primitive collector in Dixon who wanted to come out and look around. I thought what an experienced dealer had told me at the sale after I had bought the whirligig, "Dan, you've bought yourself a $750 whirligig. That is what I was waiting to bid on, but suddenly I got hungry and you bought it while I was gone."

With this in mind, I had the rare whirligig lying out on my kitchen table when the collector came. He immediately asked what my price was, and I told him, "$750."

My collector said he didn't have this much money in the bank, but he could pay $500. He begged, telling me if I sold it to him for this price he'd build his collection around it and would NEVER sell it.

I thought a bit, and recalling all the business he'd given me over the years I relented on the one condition that he keep the rarity.

He wrote the check, and some weeks went by, perhaps three, when I was told that the collector had sold my "Blackman" whirligig for $2,000 to a dealer in Sterling, Illinois. Before long I visited this man's home. He told me that he had researched the history of my former great American primitive whirligig and found it was carved in Ohio, Illinois, a town 20 miles south of here. He sent it to a large auction house along the southeast coast, where it sold for $4,000 plus.

Now Sotheby's recent catalogue on American primitives has revealed that my footless Blackman whirligig carving resold at an unbelievable $25,000 to no doubt a very wealthy American folk art collector.

When I talked to my old customer about the whirligig, he hung his head when I reminded him he had promised not to sell it. He did not deny that his selling price was $2,000, or $1,500 profit for less than two weeks' ownership. Needless to say, I am sick for selling out so fast the same day I bought.

18" Blackman Whirligig, current price, $10,000-$15,000 + . One of the paddles is beating at a bee.

25

BATTLING FOR THE
NO. 1 SPOT
AT TAG SALES

Ed Elliot lived in a nearby town, and I first met him at a sale there when he was 15. He stood next to me all through the sale. At the next sale where we met, I said, "Hey, Kid, do you want to make a little money?"

"Yes, Sir," he answered, "I sure would."

I explained that if he would do the bidding for me, it would throw everybody off track, leading them to think the antiques had less value than if I were bidding. I pointed out the antiques I wanted most and told Ed how high I wanted to go on them. He memorized this information without writing anything down or asking for any more coaching.

Thereafter at sale after sale in this town and others, Eddie was my bidder. He was paid well, and

154

I did well, too. In fact I made out like a bandit, with a kid fronting for me.

This front lasted for five or six months before the other dealers and scalpers figured out who Eddie was bidding for. They didn't have any mercy on him, then, and he had to bid top dollar to single out the antiques I had selected.

The next thing I knew, Eddie had a driver's license and an old used Cadillac. He used to come down to Dixon in it almost every day through the summer to soak in the antique atmosphere of my house. This went on for several years. Finally he began buying and selling antiques for himself, and made some good licks, all on account of what he had learned during the several years with me.

During this period, tag sales began to come on the scene, and were advertised in the paper of a nearby city. A tag sale is a sale where everything, such as the contents of a house, has been pre-priced and tagged. To have any luck at all in buying anything, you must be at the head of the line, or at least be second. This means you must be at the door of the tag sale house by 3 a.m. at the latest.

Most tag sales let in only ten at a time for ten or 15 minutes. If you are not near the head of the line, rest assured that by the time you get in, all that is good has already been bought by the pros who do the tag sales for a living.

One married couple who are professional dealers have been nicknamed #1 and #2 at the tag sales because they never fail to get there in time to get the first and second entry tickets. I've heard them brag that on several occasions they have picked up

$5,000 or $10,000 profit on signed art glass that the ladies who ran the tag sale did not recognize or did not know the value of.

Most of the tag sale operators know just enough about fine antiques to be dangerous. They know the prices of everyday stuff, but get lost when it comes to something like a $20,000 high chest-on-chest. The price put on this 1780 Chippendale chest-on-chest at a recent tag sale was at first $500, but one of the heirs, knowing that his grandmother had paid $4,000 for it 30 years before, made the sale manager raise the price to $700. I got into the door in the 19th spot. The chest had been sold the minute the doors had opened to a dealer of the town who had been in the house many times buying and selling antiques over the years. He had taken turns with his mother parking in front of the house's door from the day before and all through the night to make certain that no one else could get in first and buy the valuable early American chest.

What was strange about the sale was that while a $20,000 chest on chest was marked $750, on the floor of the front parlor a cheap, American-made Oriental-style rug was tagged at $1,750.

You can see by this story what tag sales can do to the owner. He can get the short end because those who operate the tag sale are not really up on rare antiques and sell them short a good part of the time, sometimes so cheaply that when I hear about it, I cry. I cry from sheer jealousy that another dealer has scored heavily at a tag sale.

Tag sales are the bane of auctioneers, and are a far cry from a fast-paced auction where bad and

good things are all sold for top dollar in five hours.
The tag sale may drag on for three days, every day
reducing the price of all that has not been sold down
to giveaway prices on the last day.

It was at one of these tag sales that Eddie proved
again to be my right arm. Since he lived only 15
miles from the city where tag sales were often held,
I kept him up to date on what was being advertised.
One day I noticed that one of the sales offered Pennsylvania Dutch quilts. This meant they would be
early and handmade, with appliques of perhaps
green vines and tulips. If in good condition they
could retail from $500 to $700.

I called Eddie and told him what I had read.
He agreed to go to the house at midnight to be sure
no one else would grab the quilts. I had given Eddie
a good education in the quilt business over a period
of years, so he knew how to buy a quilt right or leave
it alone.

Eddie got to the house at midnight as agreed,
and around 2 a.m. a notorious lover of and dealer
in quilts arrived, too late for #1 but still in a dangerous position at the door as #2. Eddie knew that
he must find out somehow in which room in the
house the quilts were. He managed through sweet
talk, which he was famous for, to find this out. But
not only did he find it out—so did #2.

The time to open the doors had come, and
Eddie gave his #1 ticket to the lady at the door and
ran through the house at high speed hollering ''I'll
take this'' and ''I'll take that,'' pointing to a set of
Haviland and a set of Sterling. Then at top speed
he went up the flight of steps toward the bedroom

where the quilts were. Right behind Eddie came the lady dealer, and just as he approached the top of the stairs, she got hold of his T-shirt and nearly ripped it off. She then gave poor Eddie a karate chop on the back of his neck. This caused Eddie to stumble, but did not keep him from proceeding at full speed towards the bedroom where one of the beautiful quilts was hanging on the door. Eddie hollered, "I'll buy all the quilts, mark them to me," just as the other dealer charged into the bedroom.

The lady dealer then begged and cried to Eddie to please sell her just one of the quilts. His answer, of course, was a flat no.

The tag sale manager had priced the quilts from $125 to $250 each. All were signed and dated in the 1870's by their maker. There were four great quilts and Eddie had bought them all, and then brought them to me to sell for him. He showed me where he was black and blue all the way from the base of his neck down to between his shoulder blades from the karate chop.

The quilts were sold on commission for Eddie at the best prices I could get. I owed him this for all the great things he had discovered in homes and at sales and sold to me reasonably.

A midnight lineup of diehard antiquers gathers to try to be first into a houseful of juicy antiques.

26

WHAT IN HELL
IS THE U.P.S.
DROPPING OFF NOW?

Complaints have made me more nervous than walking on a heap of eggs. Many times I was tempted to throw in the towel, but the fact that I was eating three square meals a day and driving a new Cadillac every year made me listen to my "boss" at the Antique Trader based in Dubuque, Iowa, where I do the bulk of my advertising.

A lot of dealers are thought to have quit the mail order business to retire. Actually, they have been kicked out. A tab is kept by a trade paper on your good behavior as an advertiser and dealer. If you have three tabs pulled out against you because of unresolved complaints that have come to the attention of the staff, your advertising is no longer accepted, no matter how much you plead.

Here is an example of the complaints a mail order dealer must contend with:

I received a letter late in 1986 from a lady who wrote that she had noticed a chip on a cut glass vase which she had purchased from me, but only when the sunlight hit it just right. She added that she could not feel the chip with her hand, but since she could feel it with her TONGUE, she wanted to return it! The return of this vase kept me on double strength valium for some time.

Another complainer called from California on a cold January night last year about some 1880's Puck magazines I had advertised. He wanted to buy them, but insisted that all the important center pages be intact.

I told the caller I'd go out to my below-zero warehouse and check them and call him back. There were 100 of the magazines, so it took me long enough to freeze my fingers. All the center sections were there, I told the customer on my call back. He then ordered them, but squealed like a stuck pig over the phone after he received them, and demanded that I take them back. He claimed that the old Pucks hadn't any colored center sections about golfing. I caught on that he was looking only for antique golfing color prints, which in the size of a double center spread in Puck would sell for $100 each.

My customer then complained to the paper I had advertised in that I wouldn't take back the magazines. Trade papers do not want to mediate your advertising problems. Should they be brought into the fray, 99 out of 100 times you will be made to take back your antique. If complaints continue, you will get the pink slip. I have been on the verge of this two or three times, even though I have 29 years of advertising under my belt.

Another complaint came to me when I advertised a rare doll last year as being repaired down the back of her neck, price, $600. She was an $1,800 closed-mouth Simon and Halbig if perfect. A lady called me from Minnesota and said to hold that doll. She wanted it badly and would air express $600 in a cashier's check the next day. The check arrived as promised and the doll was shipped.

No sooner did the customer get the doll than I got a call from her telling me she was returning it because it was repaired more than she anticipated.

"Didn't I tell you that there were no return privileges and that when you got her she would be yours?" I asked. Then I heard a string of curse words come over the phone that even a drill sergeant could not match. The lady dealer then talked with her husband and they both agreed with me that if I would mail them $150 they would keep the doll.

However, this did not keep the peace. In another phone call the customer told me I must take the doll back for full refund or she would contact the trade paper. This she did, and the paper told me to take the doll back. I complied.

The day after my doll came back, two local ladies who sell at doll shows came to my house looking for dolls. They fell in love with my repaired doll and bought her at my original price. They took her to the Peoria doll show the next week-end. Although business was slow, they sold one doll for a good profit and that was the repaired doll.

A month later these same two ladies, who had heard the name of the dealer who had caused me so much trouble, found themselves in a booth next to hers at a doll show. My trouble-maker saw Dixon, Illinois, listed below my friends' names and asked if they knew me. The repaired doll was then discussed, and my friends informed the trouble-maker that they had sold it at a Peoria show at a good profit. I wish I could have seen the look that they said came over her face. I was glad to hear a great ending to a complaint that took weeks to resolve and nearly resulted in a pink slip for me.

Another complaint that nearly caused me to part company with my advertising vehicle had to do with a Rookwood vase. I advertised that I had an 11-inch rare vellum Rookwood vase decorated with small sailing ships in a bay. A customer mailed me $1,400 for it and I mailed it out in good faith.

Two weeks later the customer called and told me he had noticed a minute hairline crack inside the mouth of the vase, and demanded his money back. I told him he had a seven-day only return privilege on the vase, and not two weeks. He cursed me for several minutes and then threatened to get a gun and drive 1,500 miles to shoot me with it.

After we both silenced our cursing guns, I phoned an art pottery dealer in St. Louis to check on my customer. The art pottery dealer said my customer was known to have a temper and had thrown him into a pool in his new Italian silk suit. My customer had tried to sell my vase at a big mark-up at the large Chicago Hilton show and at a Columbus, Ohio show, I learned, before he decided to find some excuse to return it.

This situation resulted in a letter to the paper I had advertised in, saying that I had mailed out an expensive cracked vase. My customer was very good at letter writing. He also wrote to editors of other trade papers I advertised in. The result was that I received several letters from editors telling me to refund the customer's money, and I took notice of them and did as I was told. If I should lose my advertising privileges in my favorite trade paper, I would not be able to make a living.

Another customer wrote me from California that she was going to return for a refund a $600 pair of Burmese decorated vases that I had sold her a year before! She said she had sold them to a dealer who was disatisfied with them and had returned them for a refund, so now she wanted a refund from me, or else wanted to set her own price on them and have me mail her the difference. After a year I did not even remember what the vases looked like. This was without doubt the grossest complaint I ever had, and I refused to honor it.

Just recently a man sent me back some canes he had purchased several months before, asking me for a $500 refund. This man was a professional West Coast cane dealer and should have known that canes that were not up to par in his opinion should have been sent back immediately. Two canes came back at $150 each and the other three or four added up to $200. After he had sold all the good ones I had sent him at a fine profit, he was attempting to unload

the ones that didn't sell back on me! That just did
not work after six months.

The way I am handling complaints now is to
give refunds on all merchandise complained about
within ten days. If someone calls me up with a complaint, and I figure my goods have been in his hands
for a ten-day inspection period and they are not on
their way back, they are his to love and cherish the
rest of his life.

Now, young people and oldsters alike, if you
can put up with this every-day nutty complaint situation, then come join me in the antique mail order
business, because there are scores of real doozy complaints out there for you to deal with that I have
left out.

27

TRYING TO BE
BUYER AND
SELLER BOTH

A few years back my little partner, Nate Ross, and I were talking at my house when suddenly I remembered a response I had received to an ad placed in the Rockford newspaper over six months before. A lady had written me to say she had several of the items I was looking for.

Nate urged me to call her and make an appointment, saying he would take off from work and drive his new van just in case we found enough to fill it. You never know when half a dozen things are offered for sale in a letter if there might be a house full.

Although I had been ill and was not in the mood, I was persuaded to call Mrs. Fairlee, and made an appointment for the next morning at 10. Nate and I were about to embark on a journey that neither of us will ever forget.

When we arrived at the Fairlee house, it turned out to be a modest two-story frame house with a screened porch. It was in January and there was a lot of snow on the ground. When we got to the door we started to take off our boots, but Mrs. Fairlee amiably told us to leave them on and said the snow would not harm anything.

I noticed as we walked into the house that there was box after box piled on the front porch. When I asked what was in the boxes, Mrs. Fairlee answered, ''All model trains in their original cellophane and paper containers. I think there are 60 boxes out there, and there are 50 toy trains to the box.''

Her husband, before he died, had run a hobby shop in Madison, Wisc., Mrs. Fairlee said, and these were part of the wares she had brought back after he died.

Nate and I kept the trains in mind. We then were told there was an old brass cash register in the shed back of the house. Nate asked if he could look at it, and then the fun began. It was the large-sized one, Mrs. Fairlee said, and she would have to get $50 for it.

There was a lot of junk and boxes to move to get to the register, but Nate in his anxiety to get at it made a path through the boxes. We knew this at once to be a $450 cash register. Nate picked it up, and small as he is, carried it for about 50 feet, when suddenly he could go no further and dropped it on his foot. He was crippled for sure, I thought, but after groaning and moaning for five minutes, he got the feeling back into his toes, and once again lifted this 100-pound-plus cash register into his van.

Nate then said, "Did you see all those printer's desks over there? We can sell every one of those drawers for $10 each."

The next thing we did was empty out all the lead type from the drawers that have 20 or 30 small compartments. When we finally had them loaded there were over 50. They were all the nice-sized ones that sell for $20 plus at flea markets once they are cleaned up. People use them to hang on the wall and display miniatures.

We also saw some huge cameras in the shed, with three-foot-long black bellows and large brass-mounted lenses.

"He must have been a photographer, too," I told Nate.

We drove back to Mrs. Fairlee's house and told her the bad news: Nate had dropped the cash register and broke the marble slab.

"Well, now, what is it worth to you boys?" Mrs. Fairlee asked. Nate answered that it was worth $20.

"Go ahead and take it, it isn't doing me any good," said Mrs. Fairlee. Then Nate, still doing all the talking and hitting it off real well with Mrs. Fairlee, told her that we had removed some drawers from some old printers' desks.

"What would you say to $50 for them?"

"That's good enough for me," she answered. "Just one more worthless item out of the shed."

But when Nate asked about the cameras, she said they were not for sale. She told us her husband had collected 5,000 cameras and they were all stored in the rooms around us.

"There is a daguerreotype camera on his list,"

she said. She showed us the long list, and it was near the head of it, listed as worth $2,000 or $3,000.

"See here," Mrs. Fairlee said as she opened the room to the east of us. "See some of his collection!"

I nearly fell over and so did Nate. The cameras were stacked up level with the top of the door and the room was full. She opened more doors and it was the same way. I could believe that there were 5,000 cameras of every kind in the rooms surrounding the small living room and kitchen where she heated the house with a cast iron stove. She cooked on one of the cast iron monsters, too.

Over in the corner were post cards, Mrs. Fairlee said. I saw about ten shoe boxes full of good old ones.

"How much for the post cards?" I asked.

"You make the price," said Mrs. Fairlee.

I figured with roughly 1,000 post cards to the box I could pay five cents each or $50. Then I cut this down to $15 a box to keep things going the way they were going, and that was cheap.

The next thing I knew, Nate was on top of a pile of cameras in one of the rooms. Mrs. F. didn't seem to mind, so he just started digging. Out he came with a nice collection of Colt revolvers and a bag full of coins. The farther he dug, the more loot he found, until he had made a tremendous hole in the center of the pile. When he handed me all this, I set it down on the table where Mrs. F. could see it. Nate made a quick deal on the whole lot on the table including my post cards, boxed it up, and rushed it to the van.

I then asked if we could look upstairs. There

I found half a barrel of old baseball cards, but Mrs. F. said she couldn't sell them. They belonged to her son. She said she'd call him if we could offer enough for them. I told her I would pay $75, even though at that time I knew nothing about baseball cards.

The son when called agreed that that was a good price, so down the stairs went around 10,000 1950's and '60's baseball cards that I eventually would sell to a baseball card dealer in Florida. We were to do a lot of business with him as seen in my first "Easy Money" book, but once we rooked him good and that was the end of dealing; however it was Nate that rooked him and not I.

Next I saw aound 1,000 old railroad magazines in one of the rooms. They dated from the 1930's and '40's and were called THE MODEL RAILROADER. I had seen them in these years for $4 each at flea markets. We carried these downstairs and left with a van-load, only to come back in a few days to dig around some more in those rooms full mainly of cameras.

Everything you can think of turned out to be underneath them. There were some fine old cast iron toys that were just like new. Then we got to talking about all the boxes of trains stacked on the porch.

"Will you sell them to us, Mrs. Fairleee?" Nate asked.

"Well, I guess so, it's not good for them to be out in the weather. I think you better give me a price on them, Nate. I don't know what their value is."

"I think $300 would be more than fair," Nate

said, "since you have been so nice. I don't have any money with me. Would you trust us to load them up and come back with the money?"

"I guess so," Mrs. Fairlee said.

Nate then loaded his van with the 3,000 toy trains and everything he had dug out of the rooms full of cameras. Since I had been injured in a car accident some years before, I could not help. We left in a hurry owing Mrs. Fairleee $675. Just before we left I asked her if she would sell us the cameras when we came back. Her answer was to hand us a piece of paper her husband had left inventoring all the cameras and listing their worth. The bottom line read $50,000. I shook my head at this price. I told her at $15,000 I could make a little. She was not going to sell at the present, she said, so I picked up the last antique I'd bought while Nate was digging and we promised we'd be back in two more days, which would be on a Saturday. Nate had already taken two days off for "sick" leave in one week.

We drove back with the $675 as promised, and Mrs. Fairleee sold us all the MODEL RAILROADERS at a low price. It took Nate two or three hours to load them up. The van was once more loaded with good saleable antiques.

Mrs. Fairlee had lived humbly, and any money offered her was deeply appreciated. She wanted to get rid of some of her husband's things for a little spare money, and did not know where to sell them.

I once more made an offer on the cameras, this time offering $17,500 or about $3 each. Again she said she'd think it over and added that she had a buyer that might pay her $50,000 for the collection. He knew about the valuable cameras in her husband's collection because they'd meet in Madison and talked about them over lunch.

Well, I figured I'd given it the College Try, and anyway, I didn't have the $17,500. Nate, who was a good friend of a bank president, said he would raise the money, in case Mrs. Fairlee called, which made me feel a little better.

Nate got home with our loot and stashed some of it in his two small sheds. I made arrangements for sale of the trains by calling a dealer who had a booth at the Kane County Fleamarket. I made a date for her to come to Nate's and look over the big train collection of narrow-gauge boxed trains offered at a cheap price. The word ''cheap'' brought her out the next night. When she got there Nate had covered the floors of both his living and dining room, plus the tables and couch, with boxes of mint trains. It looked like there were 10,000 trains, when actually there were 2,200 by count.

The dealer took one look at all the trains and paid Nate $2,000 for them because she had a ready buyer. Later she told me she sold them to her flea market operator for $3,000. A nice one-day profit for her and a better profit for us.

Then I called a buyer of brass cash registers up in Wisconsin. He came down with his wife and we got $400 for our $20 cash register.

I called the Florida baseball card dealer and he mailed me up $650 for my 6,500 baseball cards. He wrote back to try and find some more. Not knowing anything about baseball cards, I had gotten my feet wet and made over $500.

The flea market dealer came back and paid Nate $1 each for the nearly 1,000 MODEL RAILROADER magazines.

When it was all totalled up, we had made $10,000. Not bad for three trips to northern Illinois and the cost of an ad that Mrs. F had waited six months before answering.

We made one more trip back to see Mrs. F, as she had a double garage that was full to the ceiling. All we could do was look through the windows. Mrs. F was no longer amiable and told us she was going to do no more selling for the present.

That summer, we heard, she held three auctions to sell the remainder of her antiques and the trains that must have been stored in the garage. We heard she got big prices for all she sold.

One day I mustered the nerve to call her and ask again if she would sell the cameras.

"They're sold," she said. "I got $50,000 for them." Bang went the receiver in my ear.

28

MY
RIGHT-HAND
MAN

My wife plays a big part in my mail order business. I have instructed her when at sales to go through every box, all of the linen, and items in the basement looking for saleable antiques. I have no time for this because I have to stick with the auctioneer and bid on what he is selling. You never know when a rare item might be stuck in with a box of junk. Fran also goes through the doilies and piles them up in the hopes they will be sold in one shot, rather than a handful at a time, when they would be more expensive.

Collections of most anything find buyers through the trade magazines. If an auctioneer decides to split up a collection, lay off.

Fran makes the rounds, even up to the attics of houses. Many times great magazines are left in attics. At one sale Fran made me a cool $1,000 by going up to an attic and spotting a large group of saleable old magazines scattered all over the floor. The auctioneer's helpers, thinking they were junk, had left them there. They didn't even mention them to the auctioneer. I had Fran bring down one or two, and told the auctioneer I'd like to buy the similar magazines scattered up in the attic. I held up a POPULAR MECHANICS and NATIONAL GEOGRAPHIC.

He hollered out, "What am I bid for the magazines in the attic?" I bid $3, and not one person raised me. A thrill went up and down my spine. Fran had done one hell of a good job scouting. There were 1,000 to 1,500 pre-1915 radio magazines that were and are still in demand, plus a score or two of old car brochures and a ton of pre-1920 POPULAR MECHANICS. There were two station wagons full.

Fran also looks over every piece of glass that I buy for chips and hairline cracks or a missing part if a bank or toy. If it has any imperfection she has me send it back for credit and quick resale.

When I buy a set of Haviland for $500 Fran has already gone through the set and let me know how many chips there are and how many of each kind of dish.

When I have bought a set, Fran goes right to work locating boxes and paper and packing it. She is a professional because she does this every day due to my ads bringing in orders for fine glassware and china. In 25 years of packing she has had only two or three pieces broken in shipping.

When the sale is over, Fan pays the bill and then

comes to me to see that I check the ticket stubs given for each article. Many times I have been charged for something I didn't buy, and this will show up in the ticket stubs.

While I have been buying, Fran has been lugging the stuff to the station wagon sometimes a block away.

When we get home from a hundred mile drive safely with Fran always at the wheel, she unpacks the car for me, and what she can't lift is left for the next day when my boys stop after work for a cup of coffee.

The next job is to go hunting cardboard boxes once or twice a week down the back alleys of stores or in back of malls. Since I was in a head-on car crash requiring total hip surgery, Fran does all the getting in and out of the car to look everywhere for the elusive and vanishing cardboard box, which has become endangered since so many stores have installed trash compactors.

The next job Fran has to do is pack all I sell, which is around 1,000 boxes of antique glass and china a year. She won't allow me to screw up a packing job.

How can you beat a wife like that?

Top, my daughters Debra and Linda and my granddaughter, Nicole. SHE IS NOT FOR SALE AT ANY PRICE!
Lower photos, my wheelman with her clematis, and relaxing after a 700-mile drive.

29

SELLING ANTIQUES—
A LABOR
OF LOVE

When a customer walks into your antique shop or booth at an antique show, let him browse around. Don't ask, ''May I help you?'' This often scares a potential customer off and he may exit because he doesn't want to feel obligated to buy something. Play it cool and stay put until your potential buyer asks for a certain type of antique. This is the time to go to work selling an antique, although there is only a 50-50 chance that what is being asked for will be bought.

Never come on with high pressure sales tactics. What used to work 50 years ago doesn't work anymore.

Do your best to tell the customer all about the antique, and be sure to tell a convincing story about where it came from if you have one. Buyers love to hear the background of an antique.

A stock story of dealers about primitive furniture is that the piece was bought from an elderly lady who said it was handed down in her family and was carried from Pennsylvania in a covered wagon. She wouldn't have sold it, except that she was the last in the line and needed the money. A story like that is what dealers call Promotion and not a lie.

Daniel Boone was reputed to have owned a Kentucky rifle in the shop. A beaded flapper dress tagged at $200 belonged to Pola Negri and was bought at a sale held in Hollywood by one of the studios to make room for props. The story was typed on a slip that came with the dress but it got lost.

"Isn't it beautiful?" you must always say. Throw in more complimentary things about the dress, such as how such dresses sell for $350 in New York and California.

Don't say too much once it looks like your buyer or buyers are in deep thought after your sales pitch, or are at one side whispering to each other about the antique, trying to decide whether they can afford the antique or should dicker with you on the price. Usually the latter prevails, and the customer will ask if the dealer can do any better. I know from thousands of sales that I have made that it is best to set a price that can be cut 30% and some money still be made. Many times a cut of just a few dollars will sell the Pennsylvania primitive, and then again the buyer may ask for 20% discount, never dreaming the dealer can peel off 1/3 and still make some profit.

When your customer asks for a 20% reduction,

try to get him or her to agree to 10% or 15%. If the customer will not accept this, that is the time to say, "I'm losing money on this deal, but I have some other antiques I want to buy and don't have quite enough cash, so I guess I'll go ahead and sell it at that price." This makes the buyer feel good. Buyers like to bargain with you, and when they are told you are either just breaking even or losing money, they leave happy and will come and browse around your shop or booth another time. You're happy and your customer is happy.

Don't let a potential buyer get out of your shop (unless you have been turned down on a sale) until you pull out everything that remotely resembles what is wanted from your back room or even from boxes outside in your car. Don't give up until your customer gives up and walks out the door before you can convince him or her with your downcast look that something should be bought.

While customers are debating whether to purchase or dicker, do not open your mouth until you hear, "I guess I'll take it. I've just fallen in love with it."

"I don't blame you," I say. "I love it, too, and I'm a very discriminating person when it comes to flapper dresses. You've made a good buy because even plain 1920's dresses are selling for $100 in most big cities." You must keep boosting what you've sold even after it's wrapped and put in a bag. This makes your customer feel happy and convinced that she didn't make a bad buy. You have to show a lot of enthusiasm to make a sale, no matter if it is a $10 or $500 sale. Your enthusiasm must be genuine.

If your sale hasn't worked, be polite even when you want to throttle a customer, and be satisfied you gave it a good try. Wait for the next customer, who may like an expensive antique and buy from you at the ticket price, never guessing he could have saved perhaps $100 by asking if he could buy it for less.

"Buy low, sell high," this is the lullaby that Jewish immigrant mothers rocked their babies to sleep with. You, too, should try to buy antiques low and sell them high. If you work on just a marginal basis you will never make "Easy Money."

Sometimes at an antique auction you may have been carried away and paid more than you should have. This happens to all of us. If you can't seem to sell the item at a good profit, then lower the price to cost. If it does not sell then, put it high on your shelf and forget it. Try never to sell your antique at a loss. If it stays on the upper shelf long enough, someday somebody will see it, like its looks, and buy it.

Do all or most of these things, and you will sell while others cry that business is lousy all around the show.

30

IT TAKES
ONE TO
KNOWN ONE

Early one rainy evening my partner and student, Nate, and I were shooting the breeze at my house when the phone rang. It was a caller from Rockford, Ill., with an Italian name. He said he had located over 22 Oriental rugs, and that I should bring enough cash to buy them if I thought I was interested, as the people who had them had sold their house and all that was left in it was the rugs.

I asked what kind of rugs they were and in what condition. He said they looked good, especially the 9 x 18-foot in their front room. He wasn't buying them himself because he didn't know anything about rugs. All he knew was that the owners said they were Orientals and had been in the family for over 100 years.

I told the tipster that since it was raining, we

didn't know if we wanted to drive 50 miles to see
the rugs, but we would talk it over and call him back.

The tipster's information got Nate's blood boil-
ing, and he wanted to take off right away. He told
me he would drive up and look at the rugs, and if
any good at all he would buy them for us.

I cautioned Nate that this could be a set-up to
knock the hell out of me once I got in the house
with the cash that the tipster had told me to bring.
It would take a lot of cash to buy 22 Oriental rugs,
not just $2,000 or $3,000. I was hated by Rockford
dealers whom I had not allowed to buy anything
good for years, and one might be trying to get even.
It was already 8:30 and would be 10 p.m. before we
could get to Rockford and find the strange-sounding
address.

"Don't worry," Nate said, "I'll go home and get
my gun."

I thought it over and decided I'd better not go,
since Fran had overheard the conversation and was
nixing Nate's idea.

I called back the tipster with the Italian name
I could not pronounce and told him I could not get
my hands on the cash that time of night, but could
meet him the next day after the banks opened.

"You'd better not make it any later than tomorrow, because they're moving the day after and taking the rugs with them," he said. "Meet me at 5 p.m.
at my house." As I was jotting down the address, he
asked me if the 10% finder's fee would be paid if I
bought the rugs as I had advertised in the Rockford
paper. I agreed I would pay 10% of the total amount
bought, and all was set for the next afternoon.

With plenty of cash locked up in the dash of our car, Fran and I wended our way through a rough area of Rockford. I told her I thought we had better turn back.

"Let's see where he lives," she said. Soon we broke out of the sleazy part of town and into a better section. The tipster's house turned out to be an expensive-looking brick ranch. Parked by the garage was a brand new Cadillac. As soon as Fran pulled up across the street a man came out of the house carrying a brief case. He motioned for me to come over to his car, which I did. He told me he had seen me at sales and then when he had seen my ad, decided to call me instead of allowing the rugs to leave town. He claimed he had bought all the other antiques in the house, but because he didn't know Oriental rugs from American reproductions, he had stopped there.

Then he opened his briefcase and asked me to read the contract his lawyer had written up for me to sign. It said that I was to pay not 10% as I advertised, but a 20% finder's fee.

I said to myself, what the hell, I've driven this far to buy the rugs, why not pay a little more? If it turns out they are rare, he wouldn't know it and I can probably buy them at a price to make the deal worthwhile.

After I signed the contract, my tipster told me to follow him. We followed him for a long time, back through the same badly-kept-up neighborhood, and then once more we were out of it and in an area of average homes, not too good and not too bad. The Cadillac pulled up to a two-story, unpainted old house on a corner. My tipster said he would go in and tell the rug owners I was there to buy their rugs.

I didn't know what to expect when he motioned me to come in. I wondered if I would get shot or beaten as a warning to stay out of Rockford where I'd bought most of the choice antiques for 15 or 20 years. I leaned over and whispered to Fran that if I was not out in five minutes to call the cops.

When I walked into the house I nearly fell over to see all four rooms of the downstairs covered with antique rugs of varying sizes up to 18 feet. They had seen some wear, but they all had something in their favor. They all were 1800-era rugs.

I was introduced to two old women who owned them, and I began to think this was not an ambush of any kind but all legitimate. I waved to Fran that all was OK.

I looked over all 22 rugs, and one under the bed that the tipster had missed that was the best rug of all because it was a circa 1780 family rug. It was woven by different members of one Persian family and you could see where a different weaver took over and the borders would become thinner or wider and the colors would change slightly. It was seven feet long and perfect. It had probably lain under the bed for half a century.

The two elderly ladies told me they had sold their home and were moving to Peoria where they had relatives.

I had been warned by the tipster not to say a word or ask who had bought out the contents of the house. I guessed that he didn't want me to go into this matter because I might tell the ladies that they had given away their antiques.

As I was walking through the house adding up in my mind what I could pay for the rugs, I walked past a huge doorstop next to a door that was left there by the tipster, since a doorstop was needed. When I asked if it was for sale, one of the ladies said the tipster had bought it. They told me the kitchen cupboards were full of glass, also bought by my foreign informant, who told me he did flea markets and shows sporadically. He also mentioned that he sold real estate, and it was in connection with getting into a lot of homes in this capacity that he'd see antique glass and china and ask to buy it. Often the party selling the house would sell him its contents. This is what had happened in the case of the two elderly sisters. He had cleaned them out.

I kept pacing and came to a price that I could pay to double my money. I then asked the sister in charge of the selling what she was asking for the rugs. Her answer was a snappy $12,000!

I tried to explain rug by rug that the rugs were worn, and worn rugs were hard to sell. The big, 18-footer in the front room was a fine old Sarouk, but it had been walked on so much down the middle that it nearly showed its threads.

After an hour of haggling, my $4,000 offer was accepted and I called Fran to bring the money. All the while the haggling was going on my Italian informant sat with his rear end planted on the one easy chair by the door. It was only when I'd paid that he jumped up and agreed to help me out with the rugs. With the parlor rug weighing almost 150 pounds, Fran had to help too. As we were tugging and hauling the Italian told me not to pay his finder's fee until we'd hauled out the rugs, and then to pay him outside. I suddenly knew why the crooked tipster didn't want the honest old ladies to see me pay him a fee. He had made a deal with them that he would get 20% from them, too, to locate a buyer.

The rugs made a nice display around my front room, in my office, and all over the garage. The 18-footer was kept half-way rolled up. Now was the time to get them appraised free, I thought. I called in a Chicago dealer to look over the rugs, leading him to think that they belonged to a local bank. He told me to get $12,000 for them.

My rug appraiser spent the better part of a day trying to buy them for less.

"Mr. Shiaras, the very best I can do is $6,000. The rugs are all 1780-1840 rugs but badly worn."

I finally told him I'd call the trust officer at the bank and see if he'd OK a $6,000 sale. I made a phony phone call, and came back to say the bank would accept the offer.

Then I learned it would take the buyer three or four days to come up with the money. I told him I'd give him the three or four days. Out of curiosity I asked him the origin of the rugs. He said they were Caucasians and were from northwest Persia next to the Russian border. Here some of the best Caucasian rugs were made. Mori gave me the name of each one. He was an educated Persian gentleman who wore fine clothes and was not like other

Persians I had done business with. Mori left to go back to Chicago to try to round up the money.

In the meantime I called another dealer from a Chicago Oriental rug store to come have a look. After he saw what he wanted to see, he shook his head and said, "Mr. Shiaras, I'll give you $3,000 for your rugs. You have only one good one. The rest are not for me." He would not tell me which one the good one was, and of course I was not about to sell off at half the price Mori had offered me.

Then Nate got into the act by calling a New York dealer, telling him I had a lot of old rugs for sale.

By then time had run out for Mori. It was the fifth day and he hadn't come up with the money. On that day my good friend, the New York dealer, drove out after flying to Chicago, with a young New York buyer who could not only reweave a rug but could paint it to disguise worn spots making the rug look 100% more saleable. He could restore a whole rug so that you could not tell if had been repaired if you were an average American.

After Simon had looked the rugs over, and I told him that the bank had appraised them for $12,000, he and his buddy just shook their heads. After three hours of bargaining Simon told me he would pay me $6,000. I figured I'd better accept this offer, since Mori had not come back.

As the rugs were being loaded, I asked Simon which one was the best one. Instead of pointing to the seven-foot family rug that I thought was the rarest, he pointed to a brightly colored and tightly

woven rug only 3-1/2 feet long that I'd hung along
the garage wall.

"This one is worth $1,000, Mr. Shiaras," Simon
said. "If you did not have this rug in the lot, I'd
have passed them."

What none of us knew was that Fran had taken
one of the best seven-foot rugs out of the pile to
put under her sofa. This was worth probably $600.
Thus with $6,600 worth of rugs either kept or sold,
I had made a profit of $1,800 in just a few days.

Mori called me on the sixth day telling me
he had the money. I told him I'd sold the rugs to
his friend, Simon, for the same amount.

"I'm sorry, Mori, but the bank wanted them
sold or I would have been out my 10%
commission."

"Next time, then," said Mori without getting
angry.

Simon and Mori are both Persian Jews. They
no doubt had conferred and thus bid the same bid.
There's no beating three Persians at their game. Just
take a good profit and let them make five times
that much.

31

THE HOUSE
THAT WAS
LOADED

Fran and I moved to Grand Detour from nearby Dixon in 1972. I kept advertising in several trade papers and going to a lot of antique sales to buy enough to keep my ads looking attractive. It took a lot of buying to continue in the business of a national mail order antique dealer. I never missed calling at a house when I received a letter or call saying that antiques were for sale, even though what they had was not something I could use. Almost every call brought out something else good, whether it was Grandmother's Haviland or some guns that were of no use to the owner.

In this manner my local ads paid off at a time when most people knew little about antiques in this area. When you are a hungry young antique dealer you would hardly be afraid to walk into a strange house even if you knew the Devil was inside. I had this courage back in 1973 as I used to drive by an old weathered house on Highway 2 between Dixon and Rockford, not far from my home. The house had an old spiked wrought-iron fence around it. It looked like it had needed a good paint job 50 years before, and the lawn wasn't a lawn, but a patch of weeds.

As I drove by the house almost daily, I used to reflect that the house must have been built before 1900 from its size, in the days when there were lots of children. It was the kind of house that is apt to be loaded with antiques. Occasionally I would see an old unshaven man in bib overalls out back.

There's life in that house, I would say to myself. I've got to get into it before someone else does.

Sometimes I would see the character that lived there pulling an old wooden wagon to the country store in Grand Detour, where he would buy coffee, sugar, a sack of potatoes and a slab of bacon, and other things that kept. He would pull the loaded wagon back to his run-down house and stay there for another week.

I told Fran one day as we were driving by, "Pull in beside the spiked fence, and I'll go see if he does or doesn't have antiques to sell. I have a feeling that house is loaded." I told her to keep the car motor running just in case I was not welcome. I had been tipped off that the old man was not just right.

I walked up to the front gate and nonchalantly went through the yard to the side door that faced our parked car. I knocked on the door, and a gruff, monotone voice on the other side said, "Who is it?"

I said, "I'm Dan Shiaras. I'm an antique dealer from Grand Detour, and I'd like to know if you have any old things to sell."

"Come on in and sit down," the gruff voice said.

I opened the screen door, thinking I really had it made. The sight of the wild-eyed, uncombed man standing at an old kitchen table and staring at me from under his bushy eyebrows was almost enough to make me change my mind. The kitchen table was piled with nuts and bolts. But I was greedy, and I thought I could stand the sight if it turned out he had some antiques to sell.

I sat down on an old chair, but the old man continued to stand and kept looking at me. For a minute or so I talked about the weather, and things seemed to be going along alright. I asked the old man if he had a garden planted that year, to keep the conversation going. He didn't answer.

There was a little pause, and then all hell broke loose.

"You communists in Washington are sent over here to influence our Congress so you can take over the government," the old man said in an accusing tone.

The hair began to stand up on my head. "*I'm* not a Communist!" I said, "I just live down here in Grand Detour. I'm an antique dealer. I have nothing to do with Washington."

The old man's eyes got crazy-looking under his bushy brows. He pointed his finger at me.

"Hey! You're a communist! I know it," he shouted. "All communists should be dead!"

By this time the hair was standing up straight on my head.

"You're here to make me vote your way!" the old man continued. "Don't tell me you're not a communist! I can tell it! I like to shoot communists because you guys are here to run our country!"

I told myself that it was time to make a quick exit.

The old man was making his move toward the wall where a rifle was hanging on some hooks. As he made his move, I slowly moved back toward the door, not wanting to alarm him at this point by making a break for it. But when I saw him reach for the gun, I turned and was out of the door, taking it right off its rotten hinges. I began to zig-zag for the car as in combat.

The old man had gotten to the door with his repeating rifle and didn't even have to open it to begin shooting. I felt one bullet tick my collar. But being in his 70's the old man was not what you'd call a crack shot. I must have heard the crack of 10 or 12 shots. When I got to the wrought-iron fence, I put one hand on the smooth part and vaulted over. I jumped in the car and Fran, who had heard the zing of the bullets, pulled out into the highway traffic without even looking.

I was not the only one to be shot at. A week later truckers on that highway reported having windows shot out and bullet holes in the sides of their semis. (The old man said later they made him nervous when they shifted gears going up the hill.) Sharp-shooters from the sheriff's department surrounded the house and took the old man into custody. He was never seen again pulling a wagon into Grand Detour or wading around among the weeds in his garden and lawn.

Now when we go by the place where this happened, Fran will say, "It was loaded, alright!"

*Accused by a mad-man of being a communist agent, Shiaras makes a
leap for his life.*

32

THE TROUBLE
WITH
AUCTIONS

One thing I despise is an auctioneer who owns most of the antiques that are to be sold and places two or three shills in amongst the gallery of bidders. Their job is to take turns at bidding the boss's antiques up until they've made a good profit for him. They switch side to side, and run everything up.

If they get stuck with an antique, it doesn't bother the owner. He will move all the unsold antiques to another sale.

These auctioneers come out with ads advertising estate sales, but they never say whose estate it is.

One individual I know of runs an auction service out of a resort town in Wisconsin, and employs three shills, who are scattered through the audience to protect his goods in case the bidding becomes weak. He gives each a list of how high he wants them to bid on everything before they should quit bidding and let the other guy buy. If the shills have been stuck with half of the merchandise, he simply moves it to another motel the next week and adds a few more pieces, advertising the leavings as if this were the sale of the year.

Do not leave bids with most auctioneers and expect them to carry them out fair and square by starting at the bottom and bidding like you would. In many cases the auctioneers start everything at the maximum amount you said you would bid. I hate coming back to a sale and getting a bill with the exact same bids I'd left with the crooked auctioneer.

I like an auctioneer who doesn't beg for higher prices for each and every antique. I've witnessed auctioneers harp over a piece of $5 furniture for a good five minutes. I like an auctioneer who moves quickly through his sale. In this manner he can sell 600 lots in 5-1/2 hours, while the beggar would take two or three times this long and make everyone nervous. I go only to auctions where the auctioneer knows how to move a sale along and I advise you to do the same. If an auctioneer hangs on for two or three minutes, nine out of ten times someone else beside your opponent who has just thrown in the towel will jump in the fray. An auctioneer who sells an antique every minute will make you Easy Money, while the slacker will lose you money every time.

There are auctions where it is announced that the family is in the crowd and has a right to bid. I leave when I hear this, because everything the family has been fighting over that's beautiful or collectible will be fought over again, just because they could not agree how to split it beforehand. Family members sometimes stop speaking to each other for the rest of their lives over the bidding that goes on at these sales.

Most despised of auctioneers are the ones who won't let you inspect a set of valuable Haviland dishes or glassware for chips. They say to just holler up to the heirs standing on the front steps and they will hold up a piece. They have looked it all over and found only one small chip. Seeing that the heirs are all gray-haired and over seventy, you guess they can be trusted and bid $800.

Then when you start to pack the dishes you may find 41 chips on them, like I did. I went up to the auctioneer, who was eating a sandwich after the sale, and told him about the damage. He just said, "Shiaras, if you don't like our sales, don't come anymore."

It was the same with a valuable Rubena Verde water set packed in boxes under a table which turned out to have large line cracks. You could keep them, too, even though you and another dealer had run the set to $400. Complaining immediately did not help.

I still have that water set and 40 pieces of chipped silver pattern Haviland to remind me never to go to the sales of certain auctioneers.

At most other sales you can return a chipped piece of glass or anything unsatisfactory if no more than three more items have been sold. The item you reject will be resold immediately for next to nothing. Bidders are warned not to bring an article back the next day and expect a refund, nor even an hour later.

I like doing business with auctioneers who realize it is your hard-earned money that you stand to lose if an antique is damaged. You want to come to that kind of sale.

Most auction galleries don't care if you "by" bid your own merchandise. They collect 20% of where the bidding stopped, whether the item sells or not. Only a few of the auction galleries will not let anyone by bid his own consignment.

But at some sales a buyer is made to pay a 10% buyer's premium on what he buys. This is a new wrinkle in our Midwest sales area and I hope it does not stay around long. $50 to the gallery to help pay their rent and overhead is a stiff fee to pay on a $500 purchase. It is bad enough that the gallery takes 20 or 25% out of every dollar the consignor receives.

Don't go to the city for a bargain at an antique auction. If the gallery doesn't get you with its fees, the city experts in all antique fields will fix your clock. There is no way you can break through and make a profit. One deterrent is all the bids that are left with a big auction house by absentee bidders. These bids are all executed down to the last dollar by a man with an absentee bidders' sheet. All you have to do to get on it is put down 25% of your bid in cash and then show some credential. When you tell Jerry, "I want to bid $1,000" on something and put down $250 in cash, then that is exactly how high you will bid.

One thing I have seen happen time and time again at large auction galleries, and which can be to the customer's advantage, is that the best art glass and portrait plates, game plates, and sterling silver are sold last. This can be 6:30 or 7 p.m. when everyone with good sense has left and the auctioneer is tired, and only 30 or 35 hardy bargain-hunting souls are left. Bargains are there for the taking, because the sale moves fast, the auctioneer bunches lots together and sells them as one. You can buy sterling silver flatware at giveaway prices, as well as art glass. Some of the main buyers at this time are likely to be helpers at the auction house who have their own antique shops.

The auctioneer works hard at his profession and deserves a lot of credit when he is honest. An honest sale makes you want to bid on more antiques. You know if you buy a cracked or chipped piece of glass you can return it. But these sales cannot always be found.

THE AUCTION ACTION

What some local auctioneers charge

Jerry Marrs, of Belvidere, conducts and auction in Rockford for auctioneer "Col" Richard Nelson.

Most local auctioneers base percentages on their own judgement and past experience, but here are the ranges:

AUCTIONEERS Company	Fee (Percentage of gross sales)	Cleanup & Setup	Advertising	Real Estate
Boomgarden Auction Service	Over $20,000, 15%; Under $5,000, 20-22%	Costs extra	$500.00-$600.00 flat fee	3% up to $50,000, 2% after that
Miller Auction	15-25% depending on volume and amount of work	Setup can be included or paid as flat fee; Cleanup is supervised for extra fee	Included in percentage	3-5%
Richard "Colonel" Nelson	14-16% average; Small sale, 25-30%	"Nominal fee" for setup, cleanup is free	Included in percentage	1-2%
AUCTION BARNS				
Kishwaukee Auction	25% standard (inside); More if goods need cleaning	Hauling included for estates; Add 10% for smaller groups of items	Included in percentage	7% and owner pays all expenses*
West End Auction	25% average inside; Lawn auction, 10-25% plus expenses	Hauling and setup included for inside; For lawn, this can be extra	inside, included; Lawn, extra fee	5-10%*

* Neither of these auction barns does real estate regularly

Source: The Auctioneers and Auction Barns

Courtesy Rockford Morning Star.

33

HOW NOT TO
GET ROOKED IN
SELLING AT AUCTION

There are many ways to get rooked in parting with your family heirlooms. One of these is to call on an auction gallery to send a truck over to load up everything. What I advise when the truck and loader comes, is to be sure you are given a "yellow slip" listing everything you have consigned. The yellow slip is a carbon copy list of your consignments.

I would also stay right on top of the loaders to be sure they list everything. Many of them have collecting interests. They will skip writing down toys, bronze statues, or art glass. These they place at a convenient spot in the truck so as to unload them at their homes on the way back to the auction gallery.

I have been told that many of these gallery workers own gorgeous collections of art glass or

expensive toy collections, supplied by rooking con-
signors who had faith in the truckers simply because
they worked for an auction gallery.

My yellow slip came in handy to me once when
two valuable lamps were unpaid for when I received
my check from the auction gallery. When I called
the gallery I found that the lamps had never arrived.
Somebody took them, but who?

The gallery paid for the lamps at the price I
appraised them for, since I had the yellow sheet to
back up my claim. Galleries don't want the word
to get out that they are not honest.

Fran has also preached to me that I should be
at the sale when my valuable oriental rugs, Indian
rugs, or Haviland is sold. Many auction galleries
have others besides truckers that don't like the idea
of working for just an average weekly wage. If these
individuals know you will not be at the auction of
your goods, they may switch a valuable item for an
inferior one. A $3600 antique oriental rug may be
replaced with a $200 oriental of the same size. The
expensive rug is then sold to a rug dealer on the side.

The bigger the auction gallery, the more chance
you have of getting rooked. The boss, who is usually
100% honest, cannot keep tab on all his employees,
or on all the consignments, sometimes consigned
for people in nursing homes or by banks settling
estates.

Even banks get rooked, for they trust the gallery employees to go into a house with no one there
but themselves.

These practices cheat the gallery-owner as well
as the consignee, for the gallery commission on the

switched rug mentioned above would be only $80, while it would be $800 on the expensive rug.

If you are at the auction you can raise all sorts of hell if you think some of your merchandise has been switched.

Most times it is best to sell your oriental rugs at home if you are able. Get them professionally appraised first, and then ask what they were appraised for. You can always then work your way down in price until they are sold.

I guarantee they will sell, because oriental rugs today are short in supply and the demand for them in Europe, especially Germany, has gone out of sight.

Another tip about appraisals—never sell anything antique privately to anyone before having it professionally appraised, unless you are really knowledgeable about it. You might have had it lying around the house for so long that any old price offered by a dealer will sound good. In truth you might sell it for ten or 20 times more than offered.

To sum up, always get a receipt for everything loaded up for shipment to an auction gallery, and then make sure you are at the sale of your things. Write down what everything you've consigned sells for.

A collector friend has told me, after he saw two collector friends rooked, that the only way he would allow anyone to auction off his antiques would be in his back yard where he could keep an eye on everything going on!

"Wait a minute, you guys! Where's the Handel lamp on my consignment sheet?"

34

BUYING ANTIQUES
WITHOUT
GETTING ROOKED

One place to be careful of in buying is the flea market. Here you will find hundreds of dealers who many times don't know what they're selling. They may try to sell new cranberry glass for antique cranberry glass or new Mary Gregory glass for old. It is not always a case of a dealer trying to rook you. He may be just plain ignorant. You had better be a glass specialist in buying glass, for the antique market is chock full of cheap repros.

All glass ware is being reproduced, with a lot of repro Depression Glass being circulated. Auctioneers many times advertise a sale as offering antiques when instead all they have to sell is junk repros. They don't do this deliberately. Many times auctioneering is only a sideline with these individuals and they don't know cut glass from cut crystal. You must know your stuff if you want to invest in antiques.

This is true not only of glassware but of wood products as well. A wooden pull toy, hobby horse, or carousel horse may have been carved out recently and given an old look by a professional. Just recently I was at an auction where I saw a repro hobby horse sell for $3,250. The auctioneer laughed it off when I told him that the inside of the hobby horse's leg was stamped "Made in Mexico."

Then there are the flea market dealers who consciously try to bilk the public. At one prestigious antique show I walked into the booth of a dealer whom I knew as not only high-priced but a bit shady. As I broused around I saw a board about three feet high with a tag on it that read, "This is part of the crucifixion cross of Jesus Christ, $3,500." I nearly fell over when an elderly lady walked up to the board, read the tag, and told the dealer she would like to buy it for her church! The dealer smiled and took her check and then offered to carry the part of Jesus' crucifixion cross to the buyer's car!

There is a lot of scam and fraud in the world today in the antiques community as well as everywhere else.

In picking the most profitable auctions to attend, watch for estate sales. At these sales it is often left up to the auctioneer to list the sales items on the auction bill. Many times auctioneers will overlook valuable antiques because they think they are commonplace, and will not list them on the sale bill. Thus you may find "sleepers" at these sales.

But beware of estate sales where it turns out

that 10 or 15 relatives are bidding against you for the goodies.

Sales that list owner's names are not so good, because the owners love their antiques and many times will put a current market price on them at which they must sell, or they will bid them back.

I advise all new collectors to buy Bill Shroeder's Price Guide on Antiques and carry it along at sales. Don't be ashamed to lay this price guide on your lap at a gallery or to carry it in a tote bag when you are at a stand-up house sale. It has made me a lot of money over the years, and after 57 years a dealer, I wouldn't be without it either at home or at an auction.

One thing to stay away from are the big antique sales that are advertised in all the national antique publications. Eccentrics with loads of money fly in from every part of the country to blow their money on what they collect at these sales. Sometimes they are dealers that come from "dry" antique areas of the country and they will bid higher by far than is possible for you to bid, because they don't have too many antiques in California or Washington and Oregon such as we are blessed with here in the Midwest. These dealers can pay unbelievably high prices and still double their money back home.

I hope these tips will put money in your pocket. I know they have made money for me.

35

SLEEPERS

Many novices in the antique game, when looking through the Wanted to Buy sections in trade magazines, are dumbfounded. They cannot figure out why someone would want an old-fashioned, nine-foot gasoline pump with a handle for pumping the gas up into a visible gas globe, or a pump with a globe bearing some strange name, like Eagle Gasoline.

Some of those who buy these pumps do them over until they sparkle and put them up near a garage in the front yard, where they make good conversation pieces.

Other gasoline pump fanciers put them in living rooms with brass work polished and a door to the inside workings left open so guests can see what makes the pump operate. I have sold several rare gasoline pump globes to these collectors, and I enjoy talking with them about their hobby. When I ask them where their gas pump stands, they often say, "In the middle of the living room."

There are rare gasoline pump globes that will sell for over $2,000. The average Standard Oil globe will sell for $125. The average pump with some work needed and minus its globe sells for around $500.

"Sleepers" are items that the average person does not realize are in demand, but which can make you a tidy profit because you know through reading ads where the market is.

When you read "California Perfume Co. items wanted," don't sell out cheaply. California Perfume Co. is the parent company of Avon. Talcum powder cans, soaps, and perfume bottles with this company's name are collectors' items. Look in price guides and ask around as to prices before mailing them to a buyer who invariably will pay you a low price if he can. I myself try to get by cheaply in buying something I have advertised for in a trade paper.

Antique Black Americana items are in big demand. Blacks were often made to appear comical in pre-Martin Luther King days. After the Civil Rights movement brought a change in attitude toward blacks, collectors started to buy all the ridiculous-looking Black Americana they could find and at good prices. If I had to pick one thing that will continue to rise in price for a long time, it would be pre-Martin Luther King Black Americana.

Ads requesting old fountain pens appear all through the trade papers, with some dealers saying they are willing to pay $1,000 for the Parker Snake pen. This pen has a sterling silver snake wound around the pen all the way down to the point, where

its beady eyes look out. Several pens sel'
to $500 range, such as good Wohls, Parke
Schaeffers. The rule of thumb in buying pens
resale is to stick with the names I have mentioned.
The bigger the diameter of the pen, the more it may
sell for. I call the ones I sell "fat" pens, and everyone understands what I'm selling. A fat pen with
an important maker's name on it can easily bring
$250. If there is no brand name it can bring at most
$60 to $65.

Old Christmas collectibles are in demand. A
big price can be had if you get some 1880's ball-
shaped tree ornaments. I watched a man pay $300
for several boxes of six ornaments to the box. I
thought he had gone crazy. Yes, he paid $50 each
for them and sold them right after the sale for $75
silver, $85 blue, and $95 gold. These ornaments,
made in Germany, are heavier than today's and are
constructed like the old mercury glass. They have
a cap of pewter around the hanger, and this pewter
extends down over part of the ball in irregular
fingers.

Little dried-out feather trees 2-1/2 feet tall often
sell for $175 to $200. The last two I watched sell had
little berries on them but were still advertised as
feather trees. Ugly looking, but brought one hell of
a price.

Christmas tree light bulbs in the shape of
animals or story-book characters sell for $25 each,
with rare ones bringing around $75. Eight and nine-
inch paper mache Santas sell for about $75 each,
while the five-inch felt-suited ones circa 1920 bring
$50.

If you find an unusual cast iron doorstop like a golfer and it has good paint, you can sell it for $300. There are other doorstops that dealers advertise for, paying up to $500.

Dealers are open to old cast iron toys, and if in mint condition they can bring double.

A big hobby now, while five years ago it was almost unheard-of, is corkscrews. The buyers are not so much in the market any more for a corkscrew with an elaborately carved ivory handle as they are for the mechanical corkscrew. Prices range to over $500 for good mechanical corkscrews.

"Erotica Wanted!" is a mysterious ad. You don't know if they are looking for "Playboy" or "Playgirl" magazines, or one step further. It is a long-time-running ad that has to be getting results or it would not have been placed for so many years.

"Old brass post office box doors wanted." These advertisers will pay you $10 per door, so if you have a section of 80 doors, you can expect to get $800. The buyers take them apart and make banks which retail for $25 or $30.

Old perfume bottles are the most advertised for sleeper in the trade papers. This hobby surfaced just two or so years ago. Now you can easily sell a signed Bacaret, St. Louis (France), Czechoslavakia, etc., common bottle for $50, while Lalique (France) sells for around $125 to $150, much more for R. Lalique, made prior to 1940. What they are collected for is a mystery to me. I sold 100 of them recently out of a collection. The unsigned ones only brought $15 to $20. Signed perfume bottles seem to be the collectible of the future.

What is this battle to buy a machine-made quilt, or one with holes, driving the price up to $75?

The reason for the dramatic change in prices of shoddy and machine-made quilts is that a new fad has sprung up, and this is for stuffed animals made of old quilts. I have a standing order to pay me $60 to $70 for all "cutter" quilts.

At the big Oriental rug auctions there may be 50 or 60 worn, see-through throw rugs, and a battle goes on for them. I used to wonder why until I was told by Persians that they take them to their Chicago stores and cut them up into pillow covers. They wash them and stuff them with down and sell them at a good profit. These are called cutters, too.

Keep looking for the sleepers that you see mentioned in ads. They can put dollars in your pocket.

Two Newcomb College vases. The firm was established in 1895 and its ware marked N within a C. I bought the vases at a local auction and sold them, doubling my money. Another "sleeper."

36

HOW THREAT OF A
$39,000 FINE KEPT ME
OFF THE WARPATH

It was the summer of 1987 when I travelled to an antique auction around 75 miles south of Dixon that sounded like it might offer some fine china, dolls, sterling flatware, plus much more. It was advertised as a moving to Arizona sale by an elderly couple who had many fine things handed down to them along with fine antiques they had purchased during their collecting days.

When Fran and I arrived at the sale, it was standing room only in the small hall rented by the auctioneer. Fran picked up our buyer's number which was 650. This meant that 649 antique buyers and collectors had picked up numbers earlier.

The sale got under way at noon sharp with ordinary antiques selling for five times what they were worth. I figured it would be a good time to leave because from the way the ordinary items started, there'd be no chance for me to buy anything on the center table, let alone to buy the rare Indian chief's eagle feather war bonnet that I had my eyes riveted on. I wanted this piece so bad that I could taste it. It wasn't going to sell cheap, I told Fran, but I also told her, no matter the price, I was going to own it.

The day wore on with the ring men coming closer and closer to the headdress, and then finally at 3 p.m. one of them picked it up and the auctioneer started selling, all the while telling the crowd what a rarity it was, and adding that we would never have had the good fortune to bid on it had not Mr. X and his wife decided to sell everything antique they owned prior to locating in the sunshine.

What I could not figure out was why there were no sharp bidders on it, just the locals who ran me to only $575, and there the auctioneer, after begging for more money, at last knocked it off to me.

I was so happy with my headdress acquisition that I darn near stumbled when the ring man handed it to me for Fran to take to the car and lock up. This is what I coveted and this was what I got amidst the sky-high prices all the rest of Mr. X's collection was bringing. So I told Fran, Let's get the hell out of here before we suffocate, since it was 100 degrees plus outside and 110 plus humidity inside the sardine-packed hall.

When we arrived home I got a call from a Dixon lad I know who collects all sorts of Western and Civil War lore and who had seen one of my insertions in the "Antique Trader" advertising some Indian beadwork-decorated war clubs. He asked if he could drive to my house and see them close-up.

When this lad walked in the door, the first thing he saw was the Indian headdress, which I had hung in a prominent place on purpose. He looked it over and then spit out words I never want to hear again. He told me that it was illegal to buy or sell a bald eagle headdress and that it carried a $10,000 fine. On top of this the Feds could confiscate everything in an antique flea market where it was sold.

I rather doubted this stiff fine and not being able to sell the headdress at any price, so after my customer had left I called one of the nation's best-known authorities on Indian life and collectibles. I found my customer's story was indeed mainly true. But the fine wasn't $10,000. Instead, it was $1,000 for each feather!

I counted the feathers, and there were 39 of them, which meant if I had advertised and sold the headdress and the Feds had caught wind of it, the fine would have been $39,000.

I immediately got on the phone with the auctioneering firm and asked to return the headdress for a refund. The auctioneer refused, saying I had concocted this story because I figured I had paid too much, and hung up his phone with a bang.

The next day I wrote him a nasty letter telling him if he didn't take the bonnet back, I was going to turn the matter over to the proper authorities for him to be fined rather than myself. In three days the auctioneer wrote back that he was going to talk to his lawyer about my insinuations and threats.

Then a strange thing happened. Six days later the auctioneer called back and told Fran to pack

up the war bonnet and send it back, and he would
have a check in the mail for what I had paid for
it. He had found out, too, the hard way that he had
made an illegal sale. He had contacted the sellers
in Arizona, and they had agreed to refund my
money. The 1900 war bonnet would go back to the
sellers in Arizona, who said that if they were not
allowed to sell it, they would donate it to a Phoenix
museum.

My young Dixon customer and collector had
got me out of a mess by tipping me off to the conse-
quences of selling the feathers of our national bird,
which has been declared an endangered species.
The Feds don't buy stories like you were innocent
of the legality of selling eagle feathers. Instead they
would take the bonnet, and take you to the cleaners!

Indian chief wearing the sort of headdress described in this chapter.

37

AUNTIE'S
"POOPSIE"

Looking at antique auction ads can many times be deceiving because they do not accurately list what is to be offered. On this particular week I was reading an ad that advertised "some old wooden planes."

When we arrived at the Saturday sale at Geneso, Illinois, we saw not just a few wooden planes, but a lifetime collection of over 500 from six inches to 36 inches long! They took up the counter and table space on one side of the V.F.W. building where the auction was held, and took four hours to sell.

Fran and I waited impatiently hoping the auctioneer would soon get to what we had travelled to the sale to buy. We and most of the bidders squirmed and cussed to ourselves. Not till 4:30 did the dull part of the sale for most of us end.

Another antique listed in the ad was what had kept me riveted to my chair. It was advertised simply as a Steiff Teddy bear. I sweated hard after I walked into the gallery and to my amazement saw the Teddy bear seated against the auctioneer's dais. This bear was not just another Teddy bear like I've seen sell many times in my 30 years of auction-going. This Teddy bear was a mint 1904-1910 mohair Steiff with shoe button eyes and pad feet. I asked Fran for her pocket ruler to measure the bear, and darn near fell over when laid out it measured 34 inches. My heart began to pound hard after I looked the bear over and saw the silver Steiff tag in its ear.

The chance for me to buy a $5,000 Teddy bear was in the makings, because I saw neither the Silent Wonder nor his wife, the Book-reader, at the sale. They were experts on everything old and good. I'd often see the wife reading a book while waiting to move in for the kill on a choice antique that I desperately wanted and would lose to her. Both of them attended only the Chicago Hilton Antique Shows and the most prestigious shows which had a clientele of big bucks people to whom money was no object. These dealers would double their money even though I'd run them through the roof on what they bought away from me.

The Silent Wonder would have perused the whole auction, picking up and examining anything that appealed to him and to me and turning it upside down and sideways to see if it was either signed or botched up. He made me nervous examining all the goodies, and then he'd huddle with the Book-reader and they'd make their plans on what to buy.

I had prayed from around noon to 4:30 that these two dealers would be doing an antique show in Atlantic City or Cincinnati and not appear to queer my chances on the Teddy bear, which is one of my favorites in the antique field.

When the last wooden plane was sold at 4:30, the two dealers had not appeared. Due to my asking the ring man to sell the Steiff first, he held it up, and the bidding started. I bid slowly after I got past $500 so as not to indicate to the jealous auctioneers how desperately I wanted to be the new owner. $25 and $50 raises in the bidding finally slowed up at $1,200! I damn near had the bear bought when one of the family standing near the back was coaxed by the auctioneer to raise me $50. Back and forth we went with the bidding until $1,400 was bid by the heir. I calmly waited, not to alert the auctioneer as to how nervous I was, and raised the bid $25 to $1,425. After more begging by the auctioneer, the bear was finally sold to me.

I remained cool, although my heart was pounding that I had captured the rarest mint Steiff bear that has turned up at an auction in this country for many years. I told Fran to pick the bear up and take it to the car and be sure to lock it up, because there are dealers who would not hesitate to steal it if the doors were unlocked.

I drove back the 60 miles to Grand Detour with a heady feeling, knowing that I hadn't had any serious opposition in my buying, and all the time going over in my mind what one of the heirs had told Fran as we passed them while exiting the sale. The heir told Fran that her aunt in Colorado who had passed away would always keep "the darling Teddy" in a small child's rocker when they'd visit and would not allow children to pick it up, only pat it on the head and call it by Aunty's nickname for it, which was "Poopsie."

Poopsie no sooner was home and safely put in one of my child's collection rooms when a doll dealer drove up to buy her thing. To my amazement when the dealer saw the beautiful mint Poopsie, she wanted it. I thought, What the hell, I'll fire a high price at her and see her choke or cough. My price was $3,500.

No sooner had I spit that out than out came a checkbook and my Poopsie that I had only owned for a few hours had a new owner.

I heard later that this dealer sold Poopsie at the next doll show at St. Charles to a buyer from Germany who came to this country periodically to buy up all the A.M.-marked dolls at shows. It seems that the A.M. or Armand-Marseilles doll was the one Germany exported to this country the most, and it was the most reasonable to buy for resale to doll collectors back there.

This buyer paid $5,000 on the next weekend for my Poopsie, to take back with all the dolls he bought for auction in Berlin. This Teddy bear when sold was listed in Christie's monthly report on sales in Europe and England. I read it broke a new Steiff bear record price, selling for $6,800.

In retrospect, I should have put the Teddy aside when my doll buyer appeared, and then I could have featured it at $5,000 in one of my large "Antique Trader" ads. But there is an old saying that a bird in the hand is worth two in the bush, so instead I took the $2,000 profit for five hours' work and ran with it.

"Poopsie"—Steiff 32"—$5,000-$6,000. Excerpt from flyer below gives current prices of Steiff bears on wheels.

1) Large (no measurements given, but he appears quite sizable) brown Steiff bear on wooden wheels, ff underscored button in ear, circa 1920's, mohair mint: $800 up.

2) Steiff Bear, 19" high x 27" long, brown mohair, circa 1908, was on metal wheels but wheels missing, mohair mint, $1,000 up.

3) Steiff Bear, 16-1/2" high, on rubber covered metal wheels, wooden handles, circa 1935, mint mohair, $400.

4) Steiff Bear, 17" high, 24" long. ff underscored button in ear, shoe button eyes, on iron wheels with 6 spokes, mint mohair, an early piece (pre 1915). $1,700.

38

THE
GOING-WEST
LETTERS

Without sales of any consequence in our area that weekend three years ago, we decided to drive to the Randall auction at Rockton, just north of Rockford. When we pulled up to the house, I could see there were some definite possibilities. The house of native limestone was one of the oldest in Rockton and had an iron plaque planted in front bearing the date 1842. In the yard there had been set up a large wood plank ring with every inch of it loaded with antiques. Not household goods, but actual antiques, many of which had not been advertised in the sale bill. Randall, the auctioneer, was an ex-school superintendent and so far was doing a sad job in his new career of managing antique auctions.

I bought a lot of antiques that day, and as I

bought them, Fran crammed them in cardboard boxes and carried them to the car. It had been a long time since we had filled up our wagon with antiques as we were doing that day, and the sale had a couple of hours to go yet.

At about that time Randall held up a small paper barrel about half full of envelopes and letters. I asked to have a quick look, and when I noticed Utah Territory and Indian Territory on some of the envelopes' cancellations, I was into the bidding for keeps. I had a lot of experience with stamp buying and selling before World War II, and I knew that what I had just seen could mean there were some cancelled Pony Express letters in the barrel, each worth a fortune.

My only opposition in bidding for the letters was two boys, who soon ran out of money, and I bought the barrel for $85. I set it down close to my leg, as I didn't want anyone getting away with it.

The next thing I knew, the two young boys were beside me asking if I would sell the envelopes to them. They told me they collected stamps and had seen there were a lot of 1-cent and 3-cent stamps on the envelopes.

I explained to them that 1-cent and 3-cent stamps no matter how old are not valuable because millions were printed. I told them it was the higher denomination stamps that they should look for, because in pre-1900 days few could afford them and few were printed. No matter what I said, the boys kept pestering me to buy the envelopes, and I finally told Fran to lock the barrel in the car.

With the wagon loaded to the ceiling we headed

out of Rockton, glad that it had been Randall who conducted the sale rather than an old-time professional who knew his antiques. Once an auctioneer explains to a crowd what something old and rare is, the bidding on it mushrooms. Randall did not explain anything, nor had he hinted there might be something rare and valuable hidden in the barrel. In only glancing at its contents, I had seen envelopes stamped with, besides Utah and Indian territory, Nevada Territory and Walker Indian Reservation, all dated in 1863. Surely there would be letters carried by the Pony Express among them!

When we got home, I looked through the letters and saw nothing but everyday letters originating in the Rockford area. I set the barrel in the corner of my garage and was half-tempted one day to throw it in the garbage.

One Saturday soon after when Fran and I were taking off for an all-day sale, I asked my boy, Greg, to go through each letter, and if he found something interesting, to lay it aside for me. For doing this I offered him $20.

When we got back from the sale, Greg had read all the letters and had found over a dozen that were in sequence and read like a diary. They were written by a young Rockton man who had left the old limestone house and gone west.

After I had finished reading the letters of David Bligh, I felt humbled and reverent. Here was a young man of 24 years daring to travel through savage Indian territory to go to a new life in which he did not know what was in store for him. The West was not the safest place in the country to go travelling—

as late as 1873 Custer and his men were killed in his Last Stand. Bligh suffered many hardships that he wrote about to his sister back in the old stone house in Rockton.

When I read in one of the first letters that it took three weeks for a 100-wagon train to cross a river and form a circle on the other side for protection, and thought of men and women travelling with babies and young children, it was then that I started to grow humble at the thought of what our forefathers did to settle our country.

I advertised the letters in a trade paper, including in my full-page ad a paragraph condensed from the letters, headed "Bligh's account of going west in the 1860's on a wagon train." A collector of just such accounts of the early West answered my ad with a phone call. He followed this up with a letter, and by the letterhead I could see he was a collector and not a dealer because he owned a Cadillac agency in Virginia.

I wrote back a long description detailing how many letters there were and how legible. I put a $1000 price tag, or $100 a letter, on them.

The price did not phase my buyer. He called me once more and said he was sending a cashier's check. He said he couldn't wait to read them and that is why he didn't mail me his personal check because he knew I would wait for that to clear. I have made it my announced policy to hold up shipments on antiques ordered over $300 until checks clear. Once I've done business with a customer and see that his checks are good, then I ship immediately after payment with personal checks.

We sent the Bligh letters out by registered mail, and in no time at all a letter arrived from Charleston, Virginia, in which my buyer wrote that the letters made a splendid addition to his collection having to do with early western exploration and containing diaries and letters. He told me if I ever found any more, not to advertise them but to phone him collect.

The finding of the Bligh letters was an important milestone in my life as an antique mail order dealer, as I had realized my dream of finding authentic letters or a diary describing settling of the West. I was destined to run across one more such historic document, this time about the Civil War, at a sale in 1986.

Here are excerpts from the "Going West" letters:

FROM DAVID BLIGH TO HIS SISTER, ADELIA ABBOTT

Council Bluffs, Ia.
May 6, 1863

Dear Sister:

We arrived here yesterday and we are going to go across the River tomorrow and then the next station is Salt Lake about 1200 mi.

I have had good health, not even had a cold. We have past through some nice little towns, and some wild country, without a house from 10 to 15 miles and prairies 30 miles long.

There is about 300 wagons here now and they have been crossing the River for the last three weeks and they are passing where we are camped all the time.

Direct your next letter to Great Salt Lake City, Utah Territory.

Your brother, R. H. Bligh

Utah Territory
June 28, 1863

Dear Sister:

The (wagon) train is a laying over today, so I thought
I would let you know I am engaging the best of health.

The City is about as big as Beloit but is made of
dried clay. Every lot is full of peach trees and they are
loaded with fruit.

When we got to the City we had plenty of ice cream
and strawberries. The Mormons are pretty smart folks.
The night before we got to the city me and a young
school master went up to a mormon and stayed there
awhile and we had a long talk with him. He was a strong
mormon.

We got to talking about having more than one wife
and he said that he was agoin to have more when he got
so he could support them and his wife said that it was so
pleasant to have four or five wives to do the work. She
said that it was too much for one woman to take the wool
and make it up into clothes.

We left Salt Lake City last Wednesday and now we
have crost the desert. We started yesterday at four o'clock
and drove all night and until 10 the next day. We are 130
miles from the City.

Ciss Ella for me and tell her to go to school and be a
good girl.

Your brother, R. H. Bligh

FROM ELMIRA BLIGH TO HER SON DAVID

Rockton, Ill.
July 26, 1863

Dear Child:

Adelia received yours bearing date June 29. I wrote a
long letter and directed it to Coucil Bluffs but have
received no reply. . .I sold the gray horse for $80 and a
few weeks ago sold Jack for $70. You cannot think how

he run down. He was lame and stiff all over. I had the barn wall rebuilt.

Orlando Butler is dead. Paulie Spurling died last week, sick only two or three days.

Adelia wants you to get your pile of money and come home and buy a farm. Ella says she will keep house for you. She is pretty smart to work for a little girl.

We all want you to write home often and we shall always answer with pleasure, some or all of us if living. I wish you to write long letters and what you are doing and all the particulars—what a long time you have been on the road, and what a tedious journey it must have been. I hope you will have your health for when a person is sick it is pleasant to be at home if at no other time.

From your Mother, Elmira Bligh

FROM DAVID BLIGH TO HIS SISTER ADELIA

Ft. Churchill, Nevada Territory
Oct. 30, 1863

Dear Sister:

I thought I would write you a few lines to let you know where I am and what I am about. I worked on a ranch about one mile below Ft. Churchill two months and received $114. Left for Carson City stade there eight days then struck a job at $3 per day for to go and take a team and take some Indians out on the Indian Reserve and stay there till they sent further orders.

I stade there ten days and they sent for me to fetch the team back to Carson City and then I went up and see the Governor and he said that he would give me $435 per month. All the work there is to do is stay on the Reserve and cook my own vittles.

I went out and killed a wild goose and had him baked for supper. It is called Walker River about 20 miles from Ft. Churchill. The river is full of ducks and geese and the trout are the nicest fish I ever saw. I shall stay there all winter.

From your brother, R. H. Bligh

Walker Indian Reserve
May 20, 1864

Dear Sister:
    I thought I would write you a few lines to let you
know I am in the land of the living and engaging good
health and hope these few lines will find you all the
same.
    I am local agent of the Walker Indian reserve. The
reserve is situated about 65 miles from Carson City.
    The house I live in is 16 by 30. There is a kitchen
with a cooking stove in it then thare is the setting room
with a small stove, then my bedroom is next. The house
is a frame one.
    I live on the top shelf—you bet I have mountains.
Trout, ducks, hairs, and wild geese, guns and
ammunition furnished free. I milk two cows. They keep
me with milk and butter.
    All I have to do when I want something is to make
out a bill and I get it. I am getting $50 per month in
gold. I think I shall get about 60 to 70 this summer. The
catch is that I don't have anything to do. I lay a bed till I
get tired of laying then get up, get breakfast and then if I
feel lazy I go and put the saddle on a horse and take a
ride.
    This is pretty good for fifty per month. It is better to
be born lucky than Ritch, I think.
    Ciss Ella for me.

> From your brother, R. H. Bligh

FROM DAVID BLIGH TO HIS MOTHER AND SISTER

Walker River Reservation
July 15, 1864

Dear Mother and Sister:
    I received your letter yesterday. This is the second
letter I have received from home, the other dated Aug. 15,
1863.
    You wished me to write my business. It is to tend to

the Indians and tell them what to do and how to do it.
They cut about 100 tons of hay. Last year we sold it
and delivered to the fort 25 miles from here.

You spoke about sending my money home. I can
get $2 and a half in greenbacks for one in gold here.
Folks that come acrost the plains this year will find
pretty hard times when they get here for there is
thousands of idle men...

R. H. Bligh

Walker River Reservation
Nov. 16, 1864

Dear Mother and Sister:
Received your letter last week. I am still stopping
on the Indian reservation. I don't know if I shall stay
on this side of the mountains or go over to California.
The Indian agent is owing me now $550 in gold.

I went to election last Tuesday where our Poles
were held. We gave Old Abe 18 majority out of 95
votes. The state of Nevada gave Abe over 2,000 majority.
This territory was accepted as a state about three weeks
before election.

There was some immigrants went through here.
Their names was Bushnell. Mr. Bushnell's first wife's
name was Hellen Mary Bligh. We came to the
conclusion that the girls and boys was second cousins
to me.

They are over in Sanomy County, Calif. I am
engaging the best of health. Tell Emily to ciss the baby
for me.

R. H. Bligh

FROM G. E. BUSHNELL TO MRS. BLIGH

Sonoma City, Calif.
July 23, 1865

Mrs. E. W. Bligh, Rockton, Ill.
Your son David is at my house sick and perfectly

helpless and has been so for the last few months, he was taken sick sometime in April and became helpless soon after, but staid there (Nevada) until about the last of June with very little medical attention. The man that brought him to San Francisco said he begged and cryed for them to bring him to me where he could be taken care of, and he took him on the overland slow freight train on his bed and brought him over the mountains.

There they took the railroad to Sacramento and then a steamer to San Francisco. There he left him and came up after me to go and bring him home about 35 miles by steamer.

I went down on the next steamer and found him in a dreadful situation. Entirely helpless, he appeared to have no use of his tongue, talked through his teeth and very hard to make out what he said.

I got two doctors to see him and both said they could cure him but it would take 3 to 4 months. They said it would be better to take him home and they would prescribe for him.

I took him part of the way on the steamer and 12 nights on the stage. Well, we washed him clean, throwed away his bed and got clean clothes on him, and he appeared a good deal better.

He wanted me to write to you and tell you where he is. He says he is not dead nor alive. He is paralized all over and very restless and part of the time delirious. He talks about his mother every day.

I got acquainted with him last fall at the reservation house and he calls me his uncle. He had not much means. He says he had $550 when he started over here but he only got here with $160. He thinks the man kept it.

I will write you again in two or three weeks.

G. E. Bushnell

Sonoma City, Cal.
Aug. 6, 1865

Mrs. Bligh:
    I wrote you two weeks ago telling you of your son
David. Well, I have sad news for you now. He died last
Sunday night at 10 o'clock. We thought he was getting
better till Friday. His appetite failed him and he kept
getting weaker till he dropt off like going to sleep without a struggle or a groan.
    He talked about you and home about every day. We
done all for him I think that could be done just the same
as if he had been one of my own family. I have three
sons grown and it took one of us all the time and part of
the time, two (to care for him).
    He is buried in Sonoma Cemetery. The funeral
services were by the Rev. Mr. Cunningham of the
Presbyterian Church. His remarks were very appropriate
for the occasion.
    I got a new coffin for him and dressed him in a nice
new suit of clothes.
    There will be some little money after paying the
expenses.

                                        G. E. Bushnell

Napa City, Cal.
June 24, 1866

Mrs. E. H. Bligh:
    I have just returned from San Francisco. I bought a
very nice gravestone of marble and it will be shipped up
to Sonoma this week with the following inscription on it:

                In memory of D. H. Runyon Bligh
                        Of Rockton, Ill.
                      Died July 29, 1865
                       Aged 24 years

The stone cost $27 and the freight will probably be $2. I will have it set when it arrives and part of a fence around the grave. It will cost about $15. I had enough of his money left to buy them.

The picture you sent looks just as he did when I first saw him on Walker River. I will send you mine when I get it taken. I am now 8 miles from Napa City. I crossed the plains last year with my family and brought a drove of mules and rented a large farm. I rented out my farm in Missouri and left there on account of the troubles. I expect to stay here until next spring and then I shall go back home. I have a large crop of grain to harvest and sell, 340 acres. I expect if nothing happens to have 10,000 bushels.

Accept my best regards,
G. E. Bushnell

The Attack on an Emigrant Train, 1856, Karl Wimar. 55-1/4 x 79 in., oil.

A rare slice of Americana

GRAND DETOUR — Antique dealer Dan Shiaras bought an old packet of Rockton auction recently and discovered he owned a rare bit of Americana account of a young man's journey west in the 1860s.

They tell of R.H. "David" Bligh, 22, leaving Rockton and joining a wagon Council Bluffs, Iowa. He travels to the Utah Territory, comes to know the votes for "Honest Abe" just three weeks after Nevada becomes a state, helps make hay, and finally crosses the Rocky Mountains to California, where he ends.

Shiaras said he has been keeping an eye out for such an account during his an antique dealer. He estimated he has attended 6,500 auctions.

The dealer said diaries and other accounts of pioneer times, particularly those with the settling of the West, are very sought after.

"They are rare Americana, the most coveted of all," Shiaras said.

He estimated the letters might bring from $500 to $5,000, depending on them.

The letters, portions of which appear below, were advertised nationally and examined by a dealer in South Carolina for possible purchase.

Sketch courtesy of Rockford Register-Star. Letters' current value is $1,000-$1,250.

39

THE
CIVIL WAR
DIARY

Around June of last year Fran and I saw in the Rockford paper an ad of a sale that sounded like the kind of ''junk'' sale we like to go to, one where there is a lot of trash and not everything all washed sparkling bright and laid out on white tablecloths. At this ''sparkling bright'' type of sale you have to ask one of the ladies working inside the ring of merchandise to please hand you the things on the inner table that appeal to you if you want to get a closer look. This can get downright boring, trying to catch their attention to hand you 30 or 40 antiques that you want to examine for identification marks or flaws.

When we got to this sale we found that everything was out on the ground in boxes or on tables, and you could take your own good time examining everything, without a whole bevy of heirs watch-

ing to see you didn't pocket something precious.
If you don't know your antiques and are just an heir
helping out, you handle each thing as if it is worth
$1,000 when actually it is only worth $2 or $3.

I enjoy watching these old ring hens while Roy
Stenzel, who runs the auction service, gives his
usual speech. He never fails to tell the crowd that
it is unlawful to pass a bum check in Illinois and
if you do this you face a year in jail. Roy says he
does not want to make a lot of trips next week to
see his friend, the state's attorney. He will accept
checks from surrounding towns but not from
Chicago, New York, Boston, or Detroit. He will take
back and resell anything that the buyer is dissatis-
fied with, but don't wait till after the sale or tomorrow. He has some sales booked for the next three
weeks, and the dates are...This recital eats up
another five minutes.

No, it is not over yet. Roy has to tell the crowd
that this is his 3,000th sale over the past thirty years.
Fifteen minutes has gone by. A lady from Dixon who
has taken a five-minute look at the sale offerings,
heads back home. Last year she found a large bunch
of paper money hidden in a book she was looking
at at one of Roy's sales. Instead of doing what 99%
of sale-goers would have done, she turned the $1,000
or more over to Roy. Roy thanked her and told her
he would be sure to get it to the lawyer who was
handling the estate.

Such finds can be part of the profit for auctioneers' helpers who often start unloading the contents of a house into the yard at 4 a.m. All sorts of
valuables turn up in the form of large and small dia-

mond rings and plain gold rings. What could be more fun than picking up a mattress and finding a pile of money under it? That was where my uncle did his banking until he died. When you are working your tail off hauling heavy refrigerators out of basements and bedsteads from upstairs down narrow stairways, you play finder's keepers. I know this to be a fact from what I have heard in attending thousands of antique auctions.

The sale I am describing finally got started after Roy's introductory speech was over. The sale was well under way when Roy got into a raft of no-good books. Roy's helper tried selling them one at a time, take your pick. This didn't work, so Roy boxed up 15 or 20 and tried to sell them at any price. When he couldn't get even a 50-cent bid, he reached down into the box and pulled out a like-new dictionary. He started to slip through its pages, asking the crowd if it realized that the dictionary would cost at least $10 or $15 new. As he ruffled its pages, he came to a sudden halt. I was standing directly in front and saw what caused Roy to spit out his cigar. He had come across a stack of crisp, one hundred dollar bills, I estimated ten or more. He quickly shoved the cash in his pocket and just as quickly told the few who saw the find that he would see that the heirs in Ohio got it.

Roy had his helper auction some other junk while he looked through all the rest of the books, hoping that lightning would strike twice. All he found was old book markers and recipes.

I thought to myself for a month after this incident that I had needed a good dictionary, so why didn't I hurry up and bid a quarter on it as I was thinking of doing? Some days you ask yourself why you ever got up.

It was near the end of this sale, just as Roy was getting to a dusty-looking desk with lots of pigeon-holes in it that was sitting on a porch, that a scholarly-looking man went up to the auctioneer's stand and asked Roy if he would sell a little book next. Roy asked what it was. Luckily, I was standing in the front row with Fran, or I never would have heard what the answer was. The gentleman said he had pulled it out of one of the pigeon-holes of the desk, and that it seemed to be the diary of a Civil War soldier.

My ears pricked up at this. I had been a paper goods dealer for ten years and in that time I had learned that anything to do with the Civil War was very saleable. The item most in demand was any diary that described a battle or battles. This little diary could not have much in it, I thought, as it was only three by four inches in size.

Even so I did not want to take a chance on losing what might be my only opportunity to acquire this most-wanted Civil War item. The scholarly gentleman was not as determined as I was to have the diary and dropped out of the bidding to let me have it at $100.

I could hardly wait to get home and read my diary. Written in faded, brownish script, it required a magnifying glass to make out some words. Many were misspelled. Other words were archaic and required looking up in a dictionary. But I soon saw that the diary fulfilled all my dreams.

It contained over 5,000 words describing the day-to-day life of a soldier and the battles he was engaged in, and described them so vividly that I felt I was there fighting the "Rebbles" beside him.

In the main battle described, the Battle of Cheat Mountain, the Union forces of which the writer was a part defeated forces of General Robert E. Lee.

After this diary-find was written up locally in a newspaper article, I had a lot of people call me who wanted to read it, but it was too fragile to let anyone handle. Since the writer came from Indiana, I knew that it belonged in that state. I called the Civil War Library in Indianapolis, and the curator immediately confirmed that the writer was a member of an Indiana regiment.

The diary now has a home in this library, among thousands of letters and diaries of Indiana soldiers. The curator wrote me that it supplies by far the best day-to-day description of the Civil War in the library's voluminous collection.

For the history buffs I will include a sampling of the contents:

E. R. Wyeth
Memoranda Book
Commencing July the 3rd, 1861
Book 1st

Book 1st 1861

July the 4th I spent in Camp Kimball Indianapolis had a visit from my friends Living in Terra Haute Ind

on the 5th Our Regiment of the 14th Ind. Vol. left camp for grafton, Va by the way of the Railroad (Central Rd) we was received along the way by cheers and at the town of Muncie Indiana the citizens gave us an ample Repast which will be never forgotten by the *Noble 14th Reg and Myself.*

On the 6th we passed through Provo, Columbus, Zenia, Zanesville and then to Bell Air which place we Reached about noon. we then reshipped our baggage over the *Ohio River* for Grafton at Night.

Sabbath July the 7th Early in the morning we passed through grafton found all the bridges well guarded against the Rebles passed on to Clarks barge which Place we reached about noon here we got our wagons and went 5 miles and camped

July the 8th at 3 P. M. we started and traveled ten miles and camped in a small Valley

9th passed through the town of Buchana which is on the Road leading from Clarksburg to Rich Mountain

10th at 7 O Clock we again started and got to a small stream and Camped at 1 O Clock at night we was alarmed by the fireing of guns the alarm Proved to be false by sentinel fireing his piece at a hog instead the Enemy

11th from Roaring Creek we started for Rich Mountain got to Rich Mountain about noon here we got our dinner, we was then about two miles of the Rebble Camp after dinner we was drawn up in line of Battle until 6 O Clock we could hear them fireing but the would not let us go over but that Night we had to lay on our arms with the expatation of having to fight in the morning

12th the Reg was up Ready for Battle but news came that they had fled during the Night, loud cheering was done by all through the Camp they brought in a Recessionest Flag we started for Beverly we went through Camp it looked most Awful the Dead was Lying thick on the ground they left 250 of their Dead Camp equipage horses and wagons and a great many prisoners were taken by our men   we got to Beverly found the Town deserted here we camped for the night here the Rebbels told them that we would Murder them and they left terrified.

July 13th in the Morning   there was 600 Rebbles come out of the mountain and gave themselves up as Prisoners of war we then took up our line of march and started up Tygarts River valley which is a fine Country   We had 8 Regiments 2 Caverly Comppanies 2 Artilery Comppanies   We crossed the River at Huttonsville where the Rebbles Burnt the Bridge in their flight. We crossed the River and went on to Cheat Mountain Pass where we camped for the Night

Sunday July the 14th   Our Reg went to the summit of Cheat Mountain to Break up a Rebble Camp but they had gone we went back to Camp tired and hungry   Passed the rest of the day in reading and writing at Camp at Cheat Mt Pass

July the 15th also spent in Camp writing letters to loved ones at home   was on guard at Night

On the 16th Struck tents at 10 O Clock to March to Cheat Mt Summit at 4 O Clock with in 1-1/2 miles of cheat River in Sight of the Alleganies 20 miles off

17th Spent in Camp part of the Reg Chopping and building Breastworks Rester (Our [illegible]) Come with us   no great excitement that day

18th   I am helping build Breastworks   we hear that the Rebbles is 20 miles of   we make great Preperations to Receive them

19th   Gorge Rutherford was shot   he not halting when Commanded by the Pickets being killed instantly   400 Rebbles passed through the Camp on their way home being let off on Parole of honor

20th   we buried Rutherford in the honors of war   Still bulding Breastworks   Our scouts bought in nothing of any Importance but took some potatoes and Beef Cot, the nothing in Camp but the 3 years question, (Enlistment was to have been for three years.)

Sunday 21st   Our scouts went to green Brier Bridge   the Caverly got 1 killed 2 wounded one mortally his name was galt of Cincinnattia Ohio

22nd   I was on guard   it rained all day   Our Scouts went 15 miles and Rested at a Rebbel Camp following the Rebbles 5 miles wounding 1 and taking 7 Prisoners.

July 23rd   Last night Capt williamson took our Comp I out to find some Rebbles leading us continually over Rough roads and through darkness until 3 O Clock Pm we halted   took a short nap   it was very cold   got up   went to a Rebble house it being Deserted we helped ourselves to 3 *stands of honey Milck Butter* loaf *Shugar* Mutton and two *horses*

24th   today the balance of our Reg Come to us it being left behind to guard Cheat Mt Pass   we feel safer now sent out a scouting *Party* and found the Rebbles within 10 miles of us

25th   is a nice day   had news from *Manasses*   today we buried one of our men   he shot himself (Manasses was a town near Bull Run.)

26th   at Camp on short rations   our scouts seen the *seces* pickets

27th   heavy Rain all day whic is plenty heve

Sunday 28th   We dressed in our best and formed in line to Receive genrl Renyolds and Gly Elder Webb Preached 2 good sermons in the afternoon

29th   false alarm last Night   Pleasant day   Capt Brackens Ind Caverly to Camp with us today

30th   fine day   Capt Coons of Company 9 took a scouting party toward the Enemys Camp also some Cavalry

31st   fair day   Scouts returned   drove in the Enemys Pickets brought in two prisoners and killed one of their Captains

August the 1st   Our company last night went out on the Pike as advance pickets thought none of our men was out but jest as we getting our stations 4 of our Calvary came dashing past us we fired into them killing one of their horses and wounding one man.

2nd   was a fine day   a Rebble deserter come in and gave himself up to us

Aug the 3rd   very hard rain all day   in the Evening Capt Lumis of the Mishigan Artillery sent two of their Cannon to us from the other Camp   we expect an attack soon

Sunday the 4th   a pleasant day   Eld Webb Preached today all very buisy

5th   hear the Rebbles are surrounded   we dont know it to be the fact but hope so

6th   Exchanged the Cannon today for two that we captured at Rich Mt   we are drilling with them today

7th   At 10 A M our Comp I went out on the Pike 4 miles as advance Pickets   it rained very hard in the afternoon and was cold at night

next Aug the 8th   25 of us went a scouting to the noted Rock with 10 Cavalrymen   when we got to Green   Brier Creeke here the Cavalry went in advance and was fireed on by the Rebbles   2 was wounded   we come back to the [illegible] Post and then and went home to Camp

Aug 9th   Our scouts went to green Brier with some Cavalry it Rained in the afternoon   they was fired on by the Rebbles killing One of Co Bs Men and wounding two of the Cavalry seriously   the died a short time

10th   I was on Guard last Night [illegible] and Rained very hard through the day 3 on a beat and our Camp a mud hole

the 11th was Sunday   Eld Webb preached   all was quiet in Camp all day

Aug 12th   Raning as usol   stayed in our tents all day   Camp a mud hole

13th   still Raining more mud than ever

14th   very Cold   the sutlers (peddlars) Come to us today all the boys is Crazy to get tickets so as they can buy of him I was among them   we begin to live again

15th   Cold in the Morning   we have drill 4 hours a day when the weather will admit   we was buisey with the sutlers when we could get the time   the 24th Ohio Reg come to us today they with some of the 14th Ind Reg went over to the noted Rock seen the Rebbles trying to flank them   they were near their Camp   Our Boys fired on them killing 2 of them and wounding one and then they Returned to Camp

16th   still cutting timber and building Breastworks and Houses and Stables the Ohio Sutler opened his stock of goods.

Aug the 17th   today we ordered to lay the bottoms of our tents with stone and have five men in a mess   our picket guard from our Comp I is myself   C long and john koopen-humer Scouts went out tonight

18th Sunday   on guard today and last night it Commenced raining 8 O Clock Rained near all day   Scouts come in they report the Rebbles within 12 miles of us   they drove in their Pickets   they tryed to flank us but our men got away unhurt   taken two horses and some small arms

August the 19th before Brekfast this morning Our advance Pickets attacked for the first time by about 300 or 400 Rebbles they tried to flank us   2 men of our men missing their way to the (word omitted) was lost but none of our men was hurt   at night an alarm was made by the Sentinel Shoot-ing at one of the Sargnts   didnt hurt him   we went to bed at tatoo but Our Comp I was called out at 10 O clock to guard the left of our Reg   it rained very hardin the morning

August 20th   Still on guard at 2 P M   the 17th Reg AR Co Com to our assistance   2 Negro Cooks had a fight got in the Guard house   Short of our Rations today. very hungry at 1 P M one of the Evansville Co Shot his hand off his name was Bettis   the Ohio surgeon took off his hand and dressed his wound

21st   Pleasant day   our Spy came and reported 1,500 Rebbles in their Camp   the 17th Reg went bck to their camp at the Pass

Thurs Aug 22nd   raining at 10 O Clock [illegible] picket gaurd got stationed   Sergent Major was with us when 2 Rebble wagons 2 men 1 Cavalryman with his horse   took away their arms   detailed two guard over them   started to the Camp had them blinded so they could not see the Camp marched them to the colonel under the tune of yankee doodle   we stayed my watch it raining all the time   night very disagreeable

29th   still on watch   a pleasant day   we was released off guard at 11 O Clock went to Camp hungry   Scouts come in about night   Scouts found the 2 missing men   come in today   out since Sunday   they was nearly starved

24th pleasant day   but cool   1st Lieut Taylor resigned today we are not sorry   on guard in the advance we elected Ed Boosier 1st Lieut   I fired on but no one hurt

Sunday the 25th   a beautiful day   received a letter from home   on guard all day but went to church and Prayer metting had a good time of it too

26th   pleasant day. still chopping and building Breastworks Part of the 25th Ohio Reg come to us today the 14th Reg out on watch all night

27th   a pleasant day   Pitched tents to move close on a line raising them off the ground and paving the streets   the Ballance of the Ohio 25th Reg come up today   Capt Foots Co come to us from the Bridge   Co F of the 25th Reg take their places

Aug 28th   rained today at 10 1/2 O Clock one of Capt Coons men shot his leg while a guard [illeg.] with him it was nearly shot off   we have to drill 2 hours a day I was on guard last night and this morning and to had. but 1 cracker 2 day very short of crackers   no coffee and no meat   scouts report the Rebbles 5 or 6,000 strong at the Rock and burnt the Bridge at green brier and also their tents very wet and disagreeable

today 29th   still raining   all my mess is writing letters today we saw a smoke and thought it was the rebbles trying to cut off our supplies   sent out a detail to see   I was among them but it proved to be the watch of the 13th Reg at 6 P M   we had dress parade   all ordered to be ready for an attact and at guard mounting in the morning   got strict orders in case there should be an attact

August the 30th   a beautiful day but it is some cooler   Gen Renyolds attended by a bodyguard of 30 Cavalry made us a visit   the Gen looks fine   we drill 2 hours a day.   the trains of wagons bringing us some clothing   all quiet in camp today   no mail today

August 31st today is a pleasant day   their 2 general inspection of arms equipage   I am watch 2 miles to guard a by road   still building Breastworks and cutting Timber

Sabbath Sept 1st   is a beautiful day   I am still on till 8 O Clock with McChesney Rirtley & Danils   About noon Martin Fox Died of Consumption his residence was near Terra Haute And he was buried   he was the first man that has Died out of company   he was buried in the honors of war no mail today at 8 O Clock we packed our thing and went to Camp from watch to be inspected with out guns and knapsacks   there was a sermon preached in the afternoon but I was not their   I wrote a letter home

Sept 2nd   a very pleasant day we drilled   Sgt Blim drilled us   gen Renyolds and Rosencranz was here with a body guard of 20 Cavalry   all quiet in Camp today except a little mail excitement

3rd Sept   a pleasant day   drill 2 hours today   all quiet in Camp

Sept 4th   we heard that Jeff Davis is dead but think it uncertain   Capt Martins Co is on watch and put in the guard house for mutiny in camp   also john Nogal for sleeping on his post

Sept Thurs 5th   still raining   the man of Capt Coons Co that shot off his leg Died he was buried in the honors of war   Capt Martins Officers and men on extra duty   we had dress Parade an awful mudy and disagreeable time but we bear it like soldiers as our course is a noble one but last night of our men shot his finger off also 1 of the 25th shot his leg both on guard

Friday Sept 6th rained a part of the day   I am on guard at the doctor's shop all night

Sept 7th   off guard at 8 O Clock   still raining

Sunday the 8th   still it raining very muddy   2 chaplin from the 24th Ohio Reg preached 2 sermons and one of the 25th Ohio Reg was buried   no excitement in camp   boys at work on fort and chopping   we put the cannons in the fort today

Sept the 9th   pleasant day   I with the rest of the boys are ordered to wash   I am buisey all day

Thursday Sept 10th   pleasant day the col ordered the reg to strike tents and build two foundations under them   all very buisey   I wrote a letter at night

Sept 11th   Still it is raining   went on watch at 8 O Clock it rained all day and Night   a man in Co B shot his hand Rebbles found to be in the rear of us

Cheat Mt
the Col sent 2 or 3 Comps their

Thurs 12th pleasant today   off guard at 8 A M yest then we heard that our wagons was attacted by some 3000 Rebbles   we was all ordered out to attack the enemy we went down and found our wagons taken and the drivers taken prisoners   there was but 50 of our Co able for duty so they could not be in the fight   we killed a great many of them none of our Comp hurt but come near being surrounded and taken by the Rebbles the Rebbles as thick as black birds Our Co took a position on the left of the road in the rear of the camp and stayed their all night as a watch Co E was on the pike in the advance was attacked lost 2 men 1 wounded and 3 missing   lieut Juno 1st Lieut was killed a Cavalryman   it is thought that their is about 60 Rebbles killed their was 12 Prisoners taken besides 2 Contrabands Nigers

Friday Sept the 13th a very pleasant day still on the alert for the enemy we changed position towards the Camp to protect the artillery which was brought down early in the morning but the rebbles did not show themselves that day only on the hill 4 miles off east of Camp we went to Camp for dinner 3rd Ohio V 13th Ind Reg II come up we was glad to see them all the Camp is alarmed by Rebbles fireing on our watch 4 companies sent down we are all in rediness 1 man in Co R shot by our men we are in our tents again but called up in the night we are ordered to sleepe on our arms we sleepe sound all the rest of the night

Sept. 14 pleasant day again all quiet in Camp again 40 or more start for provisions sent the 3rd ohio Reg and 2 Companies to guard them and the road also the 3 out of Co E come in captured 2 prisoners 1 Lieut but had to leave them while passing the Rebbles the 13th ind Reg went back to their Camp Our Co is sent on watch on the River Bank to—off the Rebbles who are on the hill 4 miles off they drive Co E in the Bridge shooting 1 of them through the hand 1 of an Ohio Co was shot through arm also one in Co F by the name of Plymole he shot off 2 of his fingers it was done by accident

Sept the 15th we are still on watch it rains hard early in the morning but it cleared up again and was a beautiful day last night the rebbles drove in nearly all our watch we are relieved off watch about 1 O Clock the rebbles are still on the hill opposite us Morens Conover of our Co is very sick today we go to bed but soon are called we was called up 2 or 3 times during the night 1 man killed in the 25th Ohio Reg and one in our reg was killed by our own men he was shot through the hed the suttlers come with their goods also Doct Clixinaes to attend to the Sick and wounded of our Reg I

Sept the 16th a pleasant day the suttlers are busyly engaged the morn by the ragged 14th but Co F and they have to go on picket to guard our right and rear in awful gloomy place we live on crackers alone some of our Co saw Rebbles

Tues 17th   still on watch last night our wagons of provisions come being guarded by [illeg.] Reg   they bring a heavy mail we are off watch at noon   all busy at stitchery   all quiet in Camp ordered to sleepe on our arms got to sleepe

Cheat Mt Sept 18

one night for a rairity

18th   still it rains it very cold   our watch on the alert for Rebbles who are all around us   Co F is in Camp   Sleepe fine as there is no excitement

Sept 19th   a lovely day our Co goes on watch on the river below the bridge for 24 hours [illeg.] not much to eat [illeg.]

Sept. the 20th   a very pleasant day   we are relieved of watch at 10 O Clock by Co D   we are very hungry   all quiet   we get to sleepe tonight

Sat 21st   raining in the morning and continues so all day we are in quarters   very cold it is an awful night

Sabbath 22   in morning it is cold and raining   some of the Reg get their overcoats our Co go on watch 4 miles from Camp   I wrote a letter home   It is pleasant but cool at night

Sept 23   pleasant day we are off watch at 4 O Clock we got some pine feathers to sleep on I got a letter from home more clothing come up tonight   no excitement in Camp

Thursday 24th   all quiet today   they give us our clothing Over coats is the long Blues   beautiful weather

Weds 25th   pleasant day   at 8 O Clock we go on watch below the bridge for 24 hours have nice weather for it no excitement in Camp except plenty of letters

Thurs 26th   very pleasant weather of watch at 10 A No 3 Regts come to Camp last night the 9th 15 ind V 32 Ohio we are ordered to cook 2 days rations we expect to attact the rebbles. the order is countermanded it rained all night 2 cannons come up.

Sept 27th   it is still raining and very cold an awful time on guard we go out for wood and get wet in our tents   all

day rained all night   Joseph Howell our suttler was crossing
a stream and the road being washed away got in the current
of the stream was swept away and drowned in the flood Kester
and Sparks go in search of him   Sleepe very cold at night

Sat 28th   still raining and very cold our Co is on Camp
guard   today they went in search of Howell   found him in
a drift about 3/4 of a mile from where he was drowned 1
man of the 15th Reg died from cold and 13 horses died all
from cold   Virgil Sparks started to terra haute with the body
of howell   it is a cold time on guard

                    Cheat Mt Summit
Sabbath 28th   we have frost and a slight freeze but it cleared
up very nice   our Co is off watch at 8 A M in afternoon
we wrote a letter home went to the fort and hear a sermon
from Chaplin of the 9th Regt Ind followed by Eld Webb of
Terra Haute Ind

30th   a beautiful day but cool we was visited by gen Renyold
the trains of wagons bring some more provisions   all quiet
in Camp today   no mail

October the 1st   Cold but clear in the forenoon the 14th Reg
mt draws 1 Pair of Pants and drawers apiece in the afternoon
we drill 1 hour after which I do some washing 17th regmt
comes up tonight

Wedns Oct the 2nd   it is still got a letter from home this
morning we get a large   gen Renyolds come up guarded by
19 cavalry 7th V 13th ind Regmts   Come up early in the
morning 9 Pieces of cannon come up 1 Co of rifles and 1
Co of Brass pieces they are between 6 and 12 pounders we
are ordered to cook 3 days of rations expect to start sometime tonight after 12 O Clock   I lay down to sleepe the rest
are busy cooking 10 the drum beats for the 32nd Ohio to
start in the advance and we get up at 12 O Clock   the 14th
Reg is followed by the 9th ind Reg they are followed by the
13th 15th and 7th Ind and 25th and 24th   the 32nd stays
at the crossroads half way it is very dark and muddy

Thursday Oct the 3rd 1861 a fine day we get to their camp about 8 1/2 O Clock we are formed in line of Battle right and left of the Road when the Artillery opened up on them 8 or 10 minits kept up a brisk fire they then shifted their position and kept up a brisk fire 4 hours   the Rebbles returned the fire with energy   they were well fortified had plenty of Art but we don't know their No they got reinforcements from 3 to 5,000 besides artillery we had 16 pieces of Art mostly 6 pounders the Rebbles being reinforced we retired having 7 killed and 13 wounded out of the Gallant 14th our loss was altogether was 20 killed and 40 wounded suppose the Rebbles loss is 3 or 400 not certain they did not fight much went in their entrenchment we being quite tired start home to camp the distance of 12 miles and when we to camp nearly tired to death   I never was so tired in my life   Lieut Col Mahan is very sick   Capt Hoot was wounded in the arm Co F turns out 70 men Gordon Judo shot his hand by accident

Oct 4th fine day   we slept last night at the rate of 2.40 a minnit this morning the artillery and 7th 9th 13th 17th In Regmt went back to Col wagners Camp and we are left with the 25th 24th and 32nd Ohio Regiments   some of our wounded die today gen Renyolds goes to Col Wagners Camp I write a letter home   all quiet in camp today

Sat 5th   we have a beautiful day   we are still sore from our tramp   I am cooking bean soup today which is quite a rarity when we can get it after dinner we gett some fine feathers for our beds and cleane out the gutters of our streets our spy comes in and reports 500 rebles killed at the Battle and 1000 wounded all quiet

Sunday Oct 6th   fine day   feel more rested had a sleepe last night all quiet in Camp today it seems more like Sunday today than it has for some time

Cheat Mt Summit
Oct 7th   it rains today   I feel about right except I had cold rains all night all is quiet
Thurs the 8th   Cold and rainy I wrote a letter home got march-

ing orders today to leave Cheat Mountain Summit strike tents at 12 O Clock and the reg takes up their line of march had a muddy time of it Campt at the foot of Cheat Mt leaving Cheat mountain having been their 2 months and 28 days

Oct Weds 9th   beautiful day   I have a head ache at 8 A M we formed our Battalion we made a bridge of wagons

Huttonsville Oct 9th 1861

to cross the river   we camped at Huttonsville our Co on guard to Night

Oct 10th a very pleasant day   the Boys feast on apples grapes and chestnuts we feel as if we had been ushered into another world as it is warmer and we can see something once more most of our brigade come to us today and the Pay master comes also   we are off duty at 6 O Clock we had dress Parade

Fri Oct 11th another fine day we drill 4 hours a day a nice place for it in Tygarts valley   I got a letter from home

Hutonsville Va Oct 61

Sat Oct 12th   sunshine today drill 4 hours a day parade at 5 O Clock Sunday

13th pleasant day busy reading and writing today received a letter from home had dress parade at 5 O Cock some of the Boys draw their blankets

Mond Oct 14th   drill 1 hour in forenoon   Wrote a letter home we draw our money have dress parade at 5 O Clock Orders not allowing furlough to Officers or men

Thurs 15th   The officers get their pay today a man was buried

Oct Hutonsville

today out of Co B he had been wounded

Weds 16th   I go on guard today at 8 1/2 A M   a rebble prisoner was brought in today dress parade at 5 P M

Thurs 17th   I am off guard   at 8 1/2 O Clock their is 10 detailed out of each Co to work the roads under Capt kelly and Lieut Linsey I sent a letter home orders at dress parade to pass out only 2 at a time no mail today

Friday Oct 18th had drill today a great deal of doubble Quicking done during drill

Sat 19th   pleasant in forenoon have to work today drill 4 hours parade at 5 P M

Sund 20   Sunshine beautiful got Letters from home   Mr Barr come from Terra Haute today brings presents from home

Mond 21st   still continuing nice weather had dress parade at 5 P M as usol

Thurs 22nd   I am on duty at 8 1/2 drill as usol   a great deal of doubble quicking during drill parade as usol

Civil War soldier lives again through diary

By Fran Swarbrick

GRAND DETOUR — "A man talking from the grave" is the way an antique dealer describes the 125-year-old Civil War diary he bought at a Rockford auction three weeks ago.

Dan Shiaras, Grand Detour, said the diary turned up at an estate auction where mostly junk had been sold for three hours in line after line of cardboard boxes.

"On the porch was an old side-by-side secretary in fairly nice condition," Shiaras said. "When the auctioneer started selling things off the porch, a man held up a small leather booklet, which he said he had found in one of the pigeon holes of the desk. He asked the auctioneer to sell it separately."

"The auctioneer asked him what it was, and the man answered 'A Civil War diary."

Shiaras said his heart began to pound because in 50 years of antique dealing and attending 8,500 auctions, he had never seen a Civil War diary for sale. He and the finder of the booklet were the only bidders, and Shiaras bought it for $100, not knowing what was in it.

"I would have paid much, much more," the dealer said, "even into four figures. It's priceless. These things usually stay in a family."

When Shiaras got his find home, he found it was a day-by-day account of the soldier's life from July 3 to Oct. 22 of 1861. The small book contained nearly 5,000 words. It was a diary of an Indiana volunteer, E.R. Wyeth, written in ink on paper brown with age.

The account is historically valuable, Shiaras said, because it adds to knowledge about two of the least-known battles of the Civil War, those of Rich Mountain and Cheat Mountain, in Virginia. They were fought in the earliest days of the war and were part of the first campaign of Southern Gen. Robert E. Lee.

Shiras said he has not yet decided what to do with the diary. He said he has contacted an Indianapolis museum, which is eager to have it.

The diary contains odd and misspelled words and many punctuation errors.

Following are excerpts from E.R. Wyeth's "Memoranda Book 1st, 1861":

July 5th: Our Regiment of the 14th IND Vol left camp for grafton VA, by the way of the Railroad. We was received along the way by cheers and at the town of Muncie the citizens gave us an ample Repast which will be never forgotten by the Noble 14th

This Civil War diary, found by Dan Sharas, is opened to the Cheat Mountain battle entry.

Reg and Myself.

(Grafton had been occupied by Union forces shortly before to ensure the protection of the nation's capital.)

July 7th: Early in the morning we passed through grafton. Found all the bridges well-guarded against the Rebbles. We got our wagons and went five miles and camped.

10th: At 7 o'clock we again started and got to a small stream and camped. At 1 o'clock at night we was alarmed by the firing of guns. The alarm Proved to be false by sentinel firing his piece at a hog instead of the Enemy.

11th: From Roaring Creek we started for Rich Mountain. Got to Rich Mountain about noon. Here we got our dinner. We was then about two miles of the Rebble camp. After dinner we was drawn up in line of Battle until 8 o'clock. We could hear them fireing, but they would not let us go over. But that night we had to lay on our arms with the expatation of having to fight in the morning.

12th: The Reg was up Ready for Battle but news came that they had fled during the night. Loud cheering was done by all through the camp. They brought in a Recessionist flag. We went through their Camp. It looked most Awful. The Dead was lying thick on the ground. They left 250 of their dead, Camp equipage, horses and wagons. A great many prisoners were taken by our men. We got to Beverly, found the town deserted. The Rebbles told them that we would murder them, and they left terrified.

July 13th: In the Morning there was 600 Rebbles come out of the mountain and gave themselves up as Prisoners of war. We then took up our line of march. We had eight Regiments, two Caverly Companies, two Artilery Comppanies. We crossed the River at Huttonsville where the Rebbies burnt the Bridge in their flight. Went on to Cheat Mountain, where we camped.

(For the next two months and 28 days, Wyeth was to stay in camp on Cheat Mountain, which Union forces were holding against Lee. Entries of that period describe occasional skirmishes, with daily guard duty, drilling, and building breastworks.)

We hear the Rebbies is 20 miles off. We make great Preparations to receive them. Nothing in camp but the three year's question (enlistment was to have been for three years only).

Very cold. The sutlers (peddlers) come to us today. All the Boys is crazy to get tickets so they can buy of him. We begin to live again.

Received a letter from home. Went to church and prayer metting. Had a good time of it. Elder Webb preached.

Camp a mud hole today. We ordered to lay the bottom of our tents with stone.

On picket. Captured two Rebble wagons two men one cavalryman. Took away their arms. Started to camp. Had them blinded (blindfolded) so they could not see the camp. Marched them to the colonel under the tune of yankee doodle.

We heard that Jeff Davis is dead but think it uncertain.

But one cracker in two days. No coffee. No meat.

An awful mudy and disagreeable time, but we bear it like soldiers as our course is a noble one.

Still raining and very cold. An awful time. Joseph Howell, our sutler, was crossing a stream and the road being washed away, was swept away and drowned.

Sept. 28th: One man died from cold and 13 horses died, all from cold.

Oct. 2: gen. Renyolds come up guarded by 19 cavalry come up early in the morning nine pieces of cannon. one Co of rifles and one Co of brass pieces. We are ordered to cook three days rations. Expect to start some time tonight after 12 o'clock. I lay down to sleep. The rest are busy cooking. At 10 the drum beats for the 32nd Ohio to start in the advance and we get up at 12 o'clock. The 14th Reg is followed by the 9th. They are followed by the 13th, 15th, 7th, 25th and 24th. The 32nd stays at the crossroads railway. It is very dark and mudy.

Oct. 3: We get to their camp about 8 1/2 o'clock. We are formed in line of Battle right and left of the road when the Artillery opened up on them 8 or 10 minits. Kept up a brisk fire. They then shifted their position and kept up a brisk fire 4 hours. The Rebbies returned the fire with energy. They were well-fortified. Had plenty of Art (artillery) but we don't know their No (number). They got reinforcements from 3 to 5,000. We retired. Our loss altogether was 20 killed and 40 wounded. Supposed the Rebbies loss is 3 or 400. We being quite tired start home to camp the distance of 12 miles and when we to camp nearly tired to death. I never was so tired in my life.

Oct. 4th: We slept last night at the rate of 2.40 a minnit. (a reference to time of trotting horses on a track) Some of our wounded died today.

Oct. 5th: We are still sore from our tramp. I am cooking bean soup today which is quite a rarity. All quiet.

(After the battle of Cheat Mountain the Union forces descended to a valley and fell back to Huttonsville, Va., which they had passed through in July. A respite followed.)

Oct. 10th: A very pleasant day. The Boys feast on apples, grapes and chestnuts. We feel as if we had been ushered into another world as it is warmer and we can see something more more.

Article about Civil War Diary, courtesy Rockford Register Star. Current price of diary, $750-$1,000.

Lieutenant General Ulysses S. Grant, photographed at City Point, Virginia, during the siege of Petersburg.

At right, Lee wearing his military sash and dress sword, photographed in 1864 by J. Vannerson of Richmond.

40

QUIT?
HELL,
NO!!

After over fifty years of wheeling and dealing in Tiffany lamps, rare Mettlach, Royal Doulton toby jugs, and everything else in the antique field, I sometimes feel like calling it quits and going fishing.

The trouble is, antiqueing becomes an addiction like drugs or alcohol, which makes it darn hard to quit. I like to dream up ads that will bring in results in both local and national papers. It's fun opening up a U.P. box and finding a great rarity inside at a bargain price. I've had everything imaginable in antiques shipped to me at my advertized buying prices, all the way from rare Mettlach and Musterschutz steins to hard-to-find Navajo rugs and beadwork. So many interesting antiques have been sent to me through the mails that I'd need a separate book to list them all. When a rarity is mailed to you at an average price, it's more fun than winning the lotto.

Going to a sale is like attending a masquerade party, because you never know what kind of goody might be hiding in a box or behind a piled-up bunch of furniture. Many times the auctioneers don't advertise these better antiques because they don't recognize them.

But bargains nowadays are harder to find because so many antique price guides have hit the market.

For the future, I see a decline in the amount of antiques that are available. The reason is that many of the oldsters passing away today have very little or anything of antique or collectible value, since they set up housekeeping in the 40's and 50's. For local antique show and flea market dealers, this means, with less and less 1910 through 1930's antiques to be bought, the shows will suffer both in supply and attendance. I feel only a select few among dealers will be doing shows in the near future.

I hear the same words from dealers and collectors alike at sales I attend. They all say, "Where has all the good stuff gone?" The "good stuff" like Stueben, Durand, Galle, and Quezal simply isn't out there, unless you are interested in $100,000 Tiffany lamps and $30,000 dolls.

If I had any advice for antique dealers and collectors, it is not to depend on doing antique shows and flea markets for income longer than three or four years from now. This goes for shops as well.

My place in the antiqueing business will be in

placing ads rather than in beating my brains out at sales. Some sales are a waste of time. Sometimes not even the things advertised are there.

You can place ads in neighboring papers and let them do the buying and selling for you. If you've been trained in every field through trial and error as I have, you can do well in spite of present conditions. When you are called to a house to buy one item that you advertised for, you may find a lot more inside that the owners don't even know is saleable. Quilts, old toys, art glass, you never know what great bargains you may run across.

This antique business is exciting, and even though I'm reaching retirement age, I think I will keep right on. I wish you the same fun in your wheeling and dealing that I have had.

Battle of Rich Mountain, July 13, 1861